Ian McKenzie's Squash Skills

Ian McKenzie's
SQUASH
Skills

The Crowood Press

First published as
Squash – The Skills of the Game in 1986 by
The Crowood Press Ltd
Ramsbury, Marlborough
Wiltshire SN8 2HR

Revised edition 1996

This edition, retitled as
Ian McKenzie's Squash Skills, 2002

**British Library Cataloguing in
Publication Data**

A catalogue record for this book is available
from the British Library.

ISBN 1 86126 495 X

Action photographs by Stephen Line.
Line illustrations by Annette Findlay.
Demonstration photographs by Dave Sherwin.

Photograph previous page: Australian Rodney Martin plays ten times champion
Jahangir Khan in the British Open final.

Dedication
To Lucy who who made it worthwhile and
Lynne who made it possible.

Acknowledgements
This new edition of *Ian McKenzie's Squash
Skills* includes a completely new fitness chap-
ter by Joe Dunbar, a researcher in Sports
Physiology at the Department of Sports
Science, St Mary's University College, Straw-
berry Hill, Middlesex.

The addition of Joe's fitness expertise, to
what has been a popular squash classic, com-
plements the squash skills emphasis perfectly and is much appreciated.

Special thanks to Dave Sherwin for his enthu-
siastic support, encouragement and expertise
with the demonstration photographs, and also
to Lucy Soutter for her patience and the plea-
sure of working with her.

Special thanks also go to World Champion
Jansher Khan and former World Champion
Ross Norman for taking part in the photo session with Stephen Line which produced the
sequence photographs.

Typeset and designed by
D & N Publishing
Baydon, Marlborough, Wiltshire

Printed and bound in Great Britain by
Bookcraft, Midsomer Norton.

Contents

	Introduction	7
1	Technique	10
2	Basic Shots	42
3	Advanced Shots and Techniques	67
4	Skills Tests	76
5	Solo Practice	79
6	Pairs Practice and Practice Games	86
7	Coaching	95
8	Tactics	102
9	Temperament	114
10	Fitness	118
11	Your Programme	136
	Useful Addresses	140
	Index	141

Ian McKenzie began his squash career as a player and coach in New Zealand. He worked with many leading players, including Ross Norman, and was Director of Coaching for the Auckland S.R.A. His extensive coaching experience includes working for both Eton and Harrow schools, county associations in England, and international associations as far apart as Tahiti and Colombia. Moving to the UK he concentrated on coaching international and county players. He has written widely on squash both as an instructional writer and as a commentator on the competitive game. His half dozen books on squash include, *The Squash Workshop* and *Beyond Basics, Excelling at Squash*.

For the last ten years he has worked as the editor of the authoritative *Squash Player* magazine and is now the publisher of the magazine.

Ian McKenzie's Squash Skills was first published in 1986 and set a new standard for practical and incisive instructional writing on squash. It became a classic and has now been revised and updated.

I have been associated with Ian McKenzie since I was fifteen, as the recipient of innumerable coaching sessions and as a friend. His knowledge of squash is admirable, both in the technical and tactical aspects.

The stages of progression in this book are very simple, and Ian both describes and illustrates them very well, moving from the basics to the more complex areas of the game. His ideas have worked for me, and I recommend this book to any player wanting to work at getting better.

Lucy Soutter
World Junior Champion 1985
Twice British Champion

I have known and played squash with Ian since I was a junior in New Zealand. He has always enjoyed the challenge of talking, thinking and writing about squash. His ideas are clear and logical, and the methods he has developed are perceptive and innovative, and well presented here.

Ross Norman
World Champion 1986
President PSA

There cannot be many people on this earth who have such a wealth of knowledge and experience to draw upon when creating an in-depth book on squash. What better way to pick up some top tips than sharing Ian McKenzie's insight into the game through this book?

Ever since I joined the professional circuit in 1987, one thing has been certain. Whether it has been in the luxurious settings of Hong Kong and British Open or the more sobering surroundings of Karachi and Bombay, Ian would be there. Studying match after match, note pad at close hand, recording every imaginable detail, building up a vast archive of information in, what looked to me like hieroglyphic form. Then afterwards, over a game of cards, (he has been known to take the odd pound from the players), able to decipher these scribbles to provide a remarkably accurate analysis of the game. It would cover tactical errors, your strengths, weaknesses and an opportunity to highlight areas to improve. Considering this I can only suggest you discover for yourself what the following pages hold. Read on.

Chris Walker
Vice-President PSA
Chief Executive BPSA
Three times European Champion
World No. 6

Introduction

This book has helped thousands of players and coaches to learn and improve at playing and coaching squash. It does not talk about squash, it tells you exactly what you can do to get better at the sport. It is practical, it's thorough and it works.

Squash is an action sport. Using this book will help you to get into action. It is full of ideas and activities. Step by step from beginner to champion it takes you through what you can do and how to go about it.

The ideas, checks, exercises, practices, sequences and programmes have been worked out over thousands of hours on court. They have been used by beginners and internationals all trying to get better at a marvellous competitive sport.

You can become better at squash. This is your guide book. (Don't sit down and read it right through – pick your racket up and read.) Try out a few strokes.

You can develop your game in a number of areas. Developing your hitting, placement, movement, tactics, temperament and fitness. We emphasize skills and start at the simplest level: connecting up with the ball. If you have a ball control problem this is where you should start. (NB All instructions refer to right-handed players.)

Chapter 1 is about technique – how to hit the ball and get control over it. It includes action ideas. These will help you get good control over your racket, your movement, and over the connection with the ball. Chapter 2 covers basic shots – where to hit the ball – using a 'guided instruction method' to take you through the basic shots and their variations. Chapter 3 covers advanced shots.

Chapter 4 introduces the progressive skills tests, with which you can measure your percentage skill exactly. With improved technique and plenty of practice you will improve on this. Chapters 5 and 6 tell you exactly how you can practise progressively to improve your skills and movement. They provide exercises, sequences, practice rules, ideas and games.

Chapter 7 is for the coach. Chapter 8, covering tactics, is about why you win or lose. It will help you play the 'right shot at the right time'. Use the checklists and rules in your game.

Chapter 9 could be called your mental performance. How well do you think on court? Chapter 10: fitness could be called your physical performance. What does fitness really mean? The progressive programmes tell you exactly what you can do to get fitter and better.

Chapter 11 describes your programme, showing how you can fit together all the things you can do to improve your game, into a sensible and well-organized programme.

Skills

With this book you can measure your skill level exactly. You can improve this level by improving your control over the ball, and your technique. With practice on technique, skills and shots your skill will improve. Use the tests to measure your level and set targets. Use the practice routines appropriate to your skill level.

Court *(Fig 1)*

The court lines are useful reference points and are referred to frequently in the text.

The dimensions of the court are 32ft (9.75m) long and 21ft (6.40m) wide, making it longer to run up and down than side to side. The furthest you can run on a squash court is the diagonal.

The front wall is very high at 15ft (4.75m) and it is one of the beginner's first jobs to be able to take full advantage of this and not to play the whole game on the bottom half of the front wall.

Racket

Your control over the racket is the key to your success. We refer frequently to the parts of the racket as outlined in Fig 2.

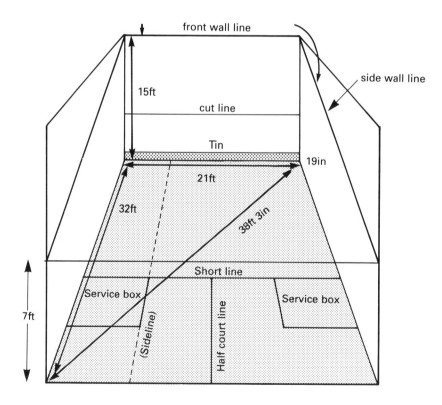

Fig 1   The squash court.

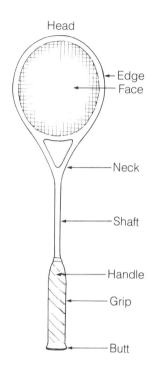

Head
Edge
Face
Neck
Shaft
Handle
Grip
Butt

Fig 2   The racket.

Playing

The motivation to improve and win at squash comes from competition. This book will help you achieve a lot by yourself, but your development also depends on how well you organize your games, targets and competitions. Joining a club can provide the competitive and social rewards. Play a variety of people including better players. Try to beat them and you will soon improve.

Coaching

This book provides a self-teaching programme. It cannot, however, analyse your individual needs as your coach can.

I have spent half my time as a coach trying to get people out of the bad habits that are limiting their game. If you have the opportunity, take coaching as early as you can. Get the basic habits right, and build your game on them.

9

1
Technique

DEFINITION

Your success as a player depends on how well you control the ball. Your technique helps to give you control. It is often called the 'basics', i.e. the basic habits on which you build your game.

Even with modern rackets which produce power easily and allow for more improvisation, the 'basics' are vital, if perhaps more easily ignored until faults become ingrained.

Squash is a form of combat. Physically we may put in a total effort to the point of exhaustion. Mentally we will fluctuate from elation to depression. The fierce competition forces us to rush. We rush in too close and spoil our shots; we try to hit the ball on the run or while twisting or falling; we snatch and flick at the ball rather than using a smooth stroke, and make mistakes and mistime our shots.

In squash we are under pressure; this often spoils technique and therefore control. This makes it more, not less, important to develop a sound technique that will give you good control over the ball and allow your game to develop without faults, limitations and bad habits.

Good technique helps give you accuracy and *consistency* in your shots.

To get good control over a squash ball you need control over your movement, your racket, and to 'time' the connection with the ball.

Aspects of Technique

In this chapter we shall look at the points of technique in turn.

1. *Ball control*: testing and developing your ability to connect with the ball.
2. *Movement control*: positioning; distance from the ball; footwork and balance.
3. *Racket control*: the V grip; the wrist; the swing, preparation and timing, and the connection of player, racket and ball.
4. *Aiming*: how we 'line the ball up'.
5. *Faults*: what can go wrong.
6. *Court movement*: getting around the court.
7. *Practising technique*.

BALL CONTROL

Ball control is the ability to connect with the ball. We often call it 'hand to eye' co-ordination. It depends on your natural ability and your learned ability. It is something you develop through practice. If you haven't played a ball sport, a racket sport or if your ball control is not very good, then you will need to do plenty of practice. Don't be discouraged because you can't run and drive the ball around the court. Get the racket and ball out and start now.

Exercise	Maximum score	Pass rate	Week							
			1	2	3	4	5	6	7	8
1	Practice exercise only									
2	20	10								
3	10	6								
4	10	6								
5	10	6								
6	10	6								
7 FH BH	10 10	6 6								
8 FH BH	10 10	6 6								
% Ball control	100	90								

Fig 3   Ball control test record chart.

The following exercises will also be useful for juniors and to get any beginner used to the racket and to the bounce of the ball.

Exercises

To pass the ball control test, you must score above the pass rate in each exercise and total above 90. Your total is your percentage ball control. Aim for 100.

1. Roll ball around racket face. Place the racket face parallel with the floor and

Fig 4   Ball control. Bouncing the ball on your racket is a simple first step in 'hand to eye' co-ordination for the beginner.

11

roll the ball round the outside of it. Practice exercise only.

2. Bounce ball on racket, continuously to twenty. Best of three attempts.
3. Bounce ball on racket above shoulder height, continuously to ten. Best of three attempts.
4. Bounce on alternate sides of racket, continuously to ten. Best of three attempts.
5. Service Start. Throw ball from hand upwards to bounce on racket face and catch again. Score out of ten.
6. Service Pat. Throw ball from hand and pat onto a wall. Score out of ten.
7. Pat. Use an underarm action and pat the ball against a wall continuously. Forehand – best of three. Backhand – best of three.
8. Volley Pat. Stand close to the wall and, using an underarm action, see how many volley pats you can do continuously.

Practise these simple exercises daily, if possible, test yourself once a week. We are now going to look at all the elements of squash technique and turn this ability to pat the ball into a squash stroke. When your percentage ball control is above ninety per cent, you are ready to get on the court and start.

MOVEMENT CONTROL

Picture a golfer quietly composed, carefully shuffling to get in just the right place, at just the right distance from the ball, in a comfortably balanced stance. If we made him stand two feet further away or two feet closer than he wished, his shot would be really awkward. If he were to take a run at the ball, the stroke would be ruined. We would expect that forcing him to play from a poor position or on the run where he may be rushed, off balance

Fig 5   World Champion Jansher Khan is a classic study in perfect balance at full stretch. Note that here on the backhand he has used the basic or closed stance. We can see that the shot will travel at right angles to the body.

and twisting his body, would affect his control and timing.

This is the sort of problem we have in squash. There isn't the time available to a squash player for careful positioning as there is to a golfer, although it is just as important. He, too, should be stopped, balanced and well set for his shot.

If you are moving, turning, twisting or falling during a shot, it will tend to be inaccurate. It is a bit like trying to fire a gun accurately while on the run. To be really accurate you must stop and take careful aim.

There are two main themes in movement control:

1. Being in the right place for the shot, i.e. positioning.
2. Being stopped and steady for the shot, i.e. balance.

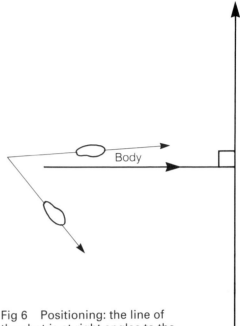

Fig 6   Positioning: the line of the shot is at right angles to the direction the body faces.

Positioning *(Fig 6)*

I often say to my pupils: 'Half the game of squash is getting in the right place for your shot'. If you are stopped, on balance, in the right place, have your racket ready and are waiting for the ball to fall down to the point where you want to hit it, the rest is easy.

The number one problem in squash is that players run to the ball. *Don't run to the ball. Move to the place you want to hit it from.* This is called positioning.

A good player is continually calculating where to move. He judges where the ball is going and then decides where he should move to and where he should wait. He moves to a different place from the ball. With practice this becomes automatic.

The action or stroke recommended to hit a ball is a side-arm throwing action.

That is, the ball is propelled at ninety degrees to the direction our body faces at impact.

One of the main ways in which we aim a ball is by positioning. Quite simply, all we need to do is get into a position at right angles to where we want to hit the ball. If the ball is too far in front, we twist or swing our bodies and often pull the shot. This means that for a straight drive the ball will come out from the side wall. If the ball is too far behind, we compensate with a wrist flick which is less controlled and less powerful than a smooth stroke.

The best positioning is where you have a slight pause while you wait for the ball to come to you. The easiest place to hit the ball is as it falls from the top of the bounce. The ball will slow here and it will be easier to judge the best impact point.

13

Distance from the Ball

If you are too far away from a ball, you may overreach and lose balance and power. If you are too close, and this is one of the main faults in squash, your swing will be cramped, you may lose balance backwards, look up during your shot and pull away while hitting.

When checking your balance, also check your distance from the ball. Is your elbow out slightly further than your front toe? Stop and check it. This is your distance check. Reach out this far, don't cramp your swing.

A useful idea when playing is to try to keep outside the 'sidelines' (see Fig 7). Of course, you will have to go inside this

area sometimes, but if you use these as a mental barrier, it will help your positioning, stop you running to the ball and straighten up your game.

Footwork

You will not automatically arrive perfectly positioned and distanced for each shot and will have to adjust your feet to get in the best place. This is footwork.

The last step is important because it gives your final position and distance but often the step before is the more important as this is the adjusting step.

Use all the different steps you can (turning, skipping, sidesteps, etc.) to get your feet in just the right place for the shot. We cover this in the movement section.

Balance

If your body is stopped and steady when hitting you have a good chance of your shot being well controlled. Your stance should provide a stable undercarriage for your upper body and swing.

I seem to have spent a large part of my coaching life saying: 'Stop for your shot' and 'bend your knees'. It is crucial that players have stopped and that their movement is not rigid or stiff. Try to develop a 'flowing', co-ordinated movement and swing. Allow movement of the knees to adjust your distance from the ball; allow transfer of weight and a strong position from which to push back to the T. Your knees are your suspension system.

At times your positioning, footwork and distance from the ball may be poor, but if you can just stay steady and balanced you can play a satisfactory shot.

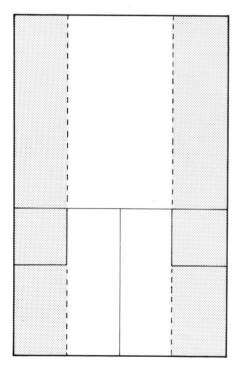

Fig 7   Keep as much of your movement outside the 'sidelines' as possible. Reach into this area.

The basic stance (also called the closed stance) provides good balance, transfer of weight and recovery, but there are several other possibilities including the back foot stance and back corner and there is not just one way to hit every ball.

Remember – the key for good movement control is to be stopped and balanced for your shot.

BASIC (OR FRONT FOOT) STANCE *(Figs 8 & 9)*

When you have read through this section, get out of your chair and go through it again. Check your balance.

1. For a straight forehand drive, face the side wall, step on your front foot (i.e. the one nearest the front wall) and point your toe directly at the side wall.

2. Keep your feet 2–2½ft (toe to toe) apart and 1–1½ft wide. If your feet are in line, you are in the tightrope walker position and can lose balance sideways easily.

3. Your back toe will point back at about thirty degrees and the ball of your foot will sit down so you can still control movement on your back leg rather than dragging your toe.

4. Bend your front knee so that looking down, it just hides your front toe. Your front shoulder should be in a vertical line with your toe and knee. Check this line: toe, knee, shoulder.

5. Shoulders should be parallel to the side wall.

Fig 8   The basic or closed stance: feet apart and wide for balance; weight forward; knees bent for suspension; body steady; toe, knee and shoulders in a vertical line.

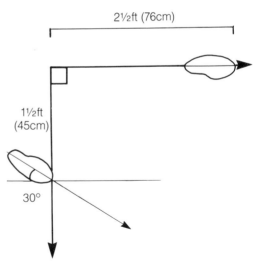

Fig 9   The basic stance.

15

6. Bend your back knee but keep your weight forward over your front foot (e.g. seventy per cent weight forward, thirty per cent back). If you bend it too much, your weight will pull away from the shot. If it is too straight, you can overbalance and twist your body.
7. Practise moving on your knees transferring your weight from your back foot to your front foot. Keep your upper body steady and perfectly balanced.
8. Try the 'push' test. Get into your stance and ask someone to push you from different directions. Can you maintain balance? Try this with your feet crossed, in line, and in the basic stance.
9. Explore the various impact points. For the forehand, this will be just behind the knee and for the backhand just in front of it.
10. Repeat the above on the backhand side.

Fig 10   The Open Stance but with the upper body turned and held still in position while the swing powers through. Note the pronation of the forearm, the concentration and the balance.

FREEZE CHECK

When practising, stop occasionally and freeze after your shot. Make a statue. Now you can check your balance, footwork, distance from the ball and positioning.

It is very difficult while hitting to be aware of exactly what your movement is like and this check, used after or before a shot, will show you just what you are doing.

OPEN (OR BACK FOOT) STANCE *(Fig 10)*

The basic stance puts the body in the best position for the shot and provides the best balance. You, however, have to step across your body and push right back to recover. This effort is usually worth it.

Sometimes when moving forward on the forehand, quickly to the side or when moving back down the court, it is quicker and easier to use the 'wrong' foot. Your footwork is not going to be perfect every time and when under pressure you'll need to hit the ball off this foot. Practise it so you can use it and be well balanced. Turn your hips and use your knees to put your body in the right place.

BACK CORNER (OR SQUAT) STANCE *(Fig 11)*

1. Point your toes into the back corner.
2. Stand evenly balanced with your feet 18in (45cm) apart.
3. Bend your knees so they move forward over and obscure the view of your toes.
4. Squat down into your stance.

This stance gives you balance over a wide range of impact points and lets you get down to the ball.

Fig 11 Scotland's No 1 player Peter Nicol prepared and solidly balanced in a back corner stance. Note the feet apart, the weight evenly balanced and the knees flexed. England's double handed Peter Marshall looks on from the T.

RACKET CONTROL

This section should be read and then re-read with a racket in your hand.

Of all the important things that a coach could say to a pupil, one thing stands out. To play a shot, the ball must connect with the racket strings. The amount of control a player has over this process is crucial.

The grip and wrist action give control over the racket head and racket face. It is the path of the racket head through the ball (i.e. the swing) that directs the shot.

V-Grip *(Fig 12)*

1. In your non-playing hand, hold the racket by the neck in front of you with the racket face perpendicular.
2. Hold your palm flat (i.e. parallel to the floor) over the racket handle and spread your fingers, i.e. you grip the racket from the top.
3. Form a V-shape between your thumb and forefinger and let this down on the top inside edge of the handle.
4. Sit the flat of the thumb diagonally along the inside of the handle.
5. The index finger fits around the handle like 'pulling the trigger of a gun'.
6. Keep a one-finger gap between fingers one and two.
7. The second joint of the index finger should sit up on the outside top edge helping keep the V-shape.
8. The remaining fingers will fit diagonally around the shaft and should be in the same line as your fitted racket grip.
9. Sit the heel of your hand just above the bottom of the handle. This is the traditional grip position, although some players like to move up the handle an inch or two.
10. Let the hand relax and smother the handle. Now hold it firmly.

This is the V- or continental grip and it is the same for the forehand and backhand.

WOBBLE CHECK

Wobble the shaft with your spare hand and check there is no movement of the racket in the hand. Look at the butt of the racket and see that it doesn't move from the heel of the hand.

17

(a)　　　　　　　　(b)　　　　　　　　(c)

Fig 12　The V grip. (a) The palm approaches the handle from above with the V shape over the inside edge. (b) The V grip. (c) The thumb diagonally along the inside of the shaft, the V on the inside edge and the knuckle sitting up on the outside edge.

GRIP CHECK

Hold the racket with the racket face vertical by the neck in your spare hand.

1. Sit the index finger half-way up the shaft with the second finger just in the top outside edge.
2. Sit the thumb diagonally on the inside of the shaft.
3. Make a clear V over the inside edge.
4. Relax your hand and slide it gently down the shaft and handle till the heel of the hand is just above the butt, keeping 1 to 3 above in place.

HABIT

The grip is your most important squash habit. Practise holding the racket at home.

1. Hold the racket by the neck. Take your grip hand off and then re-grip the racket. Repeat this ten times.
2. Use the grip check.

3. Until you have the habit, check yourself at every opportunity between rallies and games.

CHANGING YOUR GRIP

This may be a little disorientating at first but after a short adjusting period it will result in better control. Make a conscious decision to get it right, but don't expect immediate results.

Wrist *(Fig 13)*

There is an old saying in squash: 'The racket is an extension of your arm'. The grip and wrist provide the link and should give control right through to the racket head. Even with a satisfactory grip, control can be poor because the wrist does not provide the necessary firm link.

A fallacy has existed that squash shots use a 'wristy' action. This is unfortunately not a useful description and has led to rackets flapping around like propellers on

(a)   (b)

Fig 13   (a) The cocked wrist and wrist check. Keeping the
wrist up provides a strong link. Snap the racket head into
the palm to check for racket head control. (b) With a
dropped wrist control is lost.

the end of an arm. Develop a firm wrist for control of the racket head and a firm wrist action for a smooth curve on your swing.

Cocked Wrist

1. Hold the racket in front of you, relax your arm and let it point at the floor.
2. Now, using only your wrist, lift the racket in front of you until it is a little higher than parallel with the floor.

    Keep your forearm, wrist and the racket in the same line. This is a cocked wrist. It is where your wrist provides the strongest link and where you can feel your racket head.

    Hold the palm of your spare hand just above the racket head. You will be able to snap it firmly into the palm with very little wrist movement. It will feel firm and strong. This is the wrist check.

3. Without moving your upper arm, lift your forearm (i.e. hinging it on the elbow) so it is parallel with the floor.

The racket head will come to head height.

    If you turn at right angles to be in line with your shoulders, this is the backswing for your compact swing. Your racket will be making a thirty degree angle with the perpendicular.

4. Keep your arm in front in position 3 and drop your wrist to the horizontal, keeping forearm, wrist and racket in line. Keep dropping the wrist and racket. It will become harder to hold the grip firmly and obviously the control you are getting from the wrist is less. This is a 'dropped' wrist.

5. From position 3, turn your wrist and racket inwards to a right angle without moving your forearm. This is a 'broken' wrist and has less control than the 'cocked' wrist.

FEEL CHECK

Hold the racket in position 3 and think of your racket head. Imagine you have a very long light hammer and you wish to put a tack in the wall for a picture frame. Move your racket head back and forwards one centimetre at a time. Have you really got control of your racket head? This is the feel check. Use the grip check and try this again.

Ultimately you should have this feel of your racket head right through your swing.

Try the feel check in positions 1 to 5.

Racket Face *(Fig 14)*

1. With the correct grip and on your forehand side, bounce the ball up and down on your racket. Stop and hold your racket in this position. The angle of your racket head (i.e. the racket face) is in the best position to hit the ball straight up in the air. This racket face is completely open i.e. ninety degrees open.

2. What angle would you hold your racket at if you wanted to hit the ball on a forty-five degree trajectory? Obviously forty-five degrees. This may seem a lot but remember the front wall is 15ft (4.57m) high and if you were 15ft back (approximately halfway down the court) and aiming just under the 'out of court line', the trajectory of your shot would be forty-five degrees.

3. You could use a much more open racket face if you were closer and lobbing the ball.

4. Hold your racket at thirty degrees. Try a small swing with the 'line of the shot' moving up through the ball at thirty degrees.

(a)   (b)

Fig 14   The racket face. (a) The open face used to lift the ball and provide cut. (b) The closed face which will tend to bring the ball down.

5. Hold the racket face perpendicular to the floor. This is where the racket face is flat, i.e. there is no angle.
6. Turn your racket over so you could continually bounce the ball on the floor. This is completely closed.
7. Close your racket face forty-five degrees.

If during your swing you close your racket face, there will be a tendency for the ball to go down. This is called 'going over the ball' or 'rolling your wrist' and is generally a fault.

Try rolling your wrist and feeling your racket head. Is there the same control?

8. Run through the above on your backhand side.

Racket Edge *(Fig 15)*

Ken Hiscoe (the great Australian stroke-maker of the 1960s) once showed me a useful little exercise to clarify the cocked wrist, racket face and wrist action.

1. Hold the racket in front of you as in wrist position 2 for cocked wrist.
2. Take the edge of the racket head back towards the right shoulder to a position in line with the shoulders. This cocks the wrist for the forehand. You just extend this to get into your backswing position.
3. Take the edge of the racket head to the left shoulder. This cocks the wrist for the backhand.

Swing

Golfers are concerned about their swing. They practise grooving it many times before hitting, because they realize how crucial it is to have control over the ball.

The problem in squash is that we just don't have the same time and there are many other things going on as well.

(a) (b) (c)

Fig 15 (a) The racket edge: ready position. (b) Take the racket edge to the right shoulder. This cocks the wrist and opens the racket face for the forehand. (c) Take the racket edge to the left shoulder. This cocks the wrist and opens the racket face for the backhand.

Take time to develop your control over the ball, develop your swing. Develop an efficient, smooth, controlled, grooved and rhythmic action that will push the racket head 'down the line of the shot' and give you consistency and accuracy.

The squash action is a throwing action. An overarm throw is used in a smash action and an underarm throw in the patting action. If you throw side-arm, this is the squash action. You use this action when you skim a stone on a lake or in a side-arm cricket throw. On the backhand, it is like throwing a frisbee.

The squash action is a smooth curve made up of three parts – movement around the three joints – the wrist, the elbow and the shoulder.

WRIST ACTION

This should be firm, and although the wrist will uncock a little through impact it should move through and up with the follow-through thus providing good control of the racket head throughout the swing.

It can, however, range from being a 'locked wrist' (where feel and control are required), to a 'wristy' action when used to compensate for position, using 'deception' or to add power ('wrist snap').

FOREARM ACTION

The squash swing is largely a forearm action hinging on the elbow. This incorporates the 'turning' and 'hinging' actions of the forearm. Hold your hand out in front of you, palm up. Now turn it over. (This is pronation.) Now turn it back again. (This is supination.)

Put your forearm at waist height in line with shoulders and holding your elbow steady, let it turn through 180 degrees.

Practise this incorporating the turning of the arm and reverse it for the backhand.

Leaving the elbow in place and using only this action would unfortunately result in the swing rolling over the ball and bringing it down. This brings us to the full arm action which will allow the elbow to move through and add power.

ARM ACTION (Fig 16)

Hold your arm out straight in line with and at the height of your shoulders. Turn this right across your body 180 degrees. Watch your elbow move through.

Relax your shoulders. Take your shoulders back and round as far as they will go. Now swing right across your body, until your shoulder restricts the movement. This is your full arm action.

Squash Action

FROM A V TO A V

Try it! Point your arm out straight at shoulder height in line with your shoulders. Bend your elbow to make a V. Bring your elbow and the heel of your hand through. Let the heel turn to an open palm at the vertical point in front of your body. Your arm line is in here. Let the elbow go across your body and let the arm continue turning on the elbow right through to a V and over a little.

Practise this and make it a smooth rhythmic action. Start by trying it slowly without the racket. Next, progress to practising with the racket but without the ball, just like a golfer.

Compact Swing

FOREHAND (Fig 17)

1. *Preparation.* Adopt a stance facing the side wall (if on court or any wall if off court), with the racket in front of you and the wrist up. Use the feel check.

Fig 16   Power is added to the swing by the shoulder turn and the transfer of weight into the shot. Here ten times British Open Champion Jahangir Khan winds up and lunges into the shot. Note the preparation for a full swing and the shoulder turn.

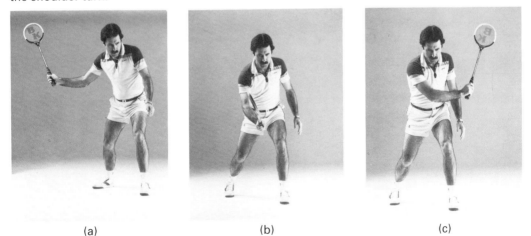

| (a) | (b) | (c) |

Fig 17   The compact swing: forehand.
(a) Backswing. (b) Impact. (c) Follow-through.

23

2. *Backswing.* Take the racket edge directly (on the shortest route) to the backswing position. Point your racket head directly at the back wall at head height (ninety degrees) and in a position in line with your shoulders. Bend your elbow so that it sits just out from your hip. Check that your wrist is cocked and your racket face is open (e.g. twenty degrees).

3. Use the feel check.

4. *Impact.* Slowly and smoothly, bring your racket down and then through to the impact point. This will be just behind the knee where the racket makes a right angle with the side wall and is parallel with the floor. The wrist will be raised just above the forearm (twenty degrees).

5. Use the feel check. This is also a good point to check the stance.

6. *Follow-through.* Continue in a straight line through the impact point and across your body to form a V. Point the racket straight at the front wall in line with and at shoulder height. The racket face will be vertical or may have closed a little on the follow-through but it must have been open on the straight part of the swing through impact. Your elbow will have come through to sit over the navel.

7. Use the feel check again.

8. Try this as one smooth and precise swing from the start of the backswing to the finish of the follow-through.

9. Practise to groove it.

BACKHAND *(Fig 18)*

1. *Preparation.* Adopt a stance facing the side wall with the racket in front of you and with the wrist up.

2. *Backswing.* Take the racket edge directly to the backswing position at the same time turning the shoulder and taking the elbow across your body and past your navel. For this exercise, rest your grip hand on your bicep and tuck the racket around behind your shoulder. (This is a definite and useful position to run through the swing from but in practice it should sit out a little further from the body, so as not to result in a cramped swing.)

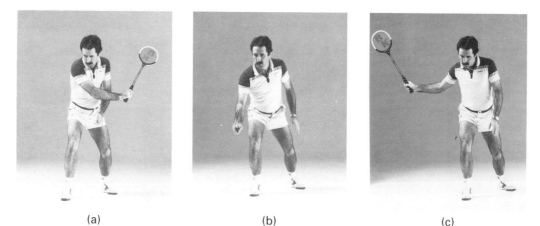

     (a)   (b)   (c)

Fig 18   Compact swing: backhand.
(a) Backswing. (b) Impact. (c) Follow-through.

3. Use the feel check.
4. *Impact.* Swing straight down and then through to the impact point. Stop just past your knee and check stance, distance, wrist and racket face.
5. Use the feel check.
6. *Follow-through.* Allow the follow-through to hinge on your elbow and swing through to a point where your racket head points straight at the front wall (ninety degrees) at shoulder height. Don't straighten or lock your arm. Let it turn on the elbow and form a V.
7. Use the feel check.
8. Try this as one smooth and precise swing from the start of the backswing to the finish of the follow-through.
9. Practise to groove it.

Racket Paths

It is the path of the racket head through the ball that directs the shot. This varies depending on the type of shot you are playing. Generally, your swing will go in a U shape with a backswing to the top of the U, then a downswing and a through swing. Impact is a point on the through part of the swing. Here the racket head is on a straight path down the line of the shot. The follow-through is the upward part.

You may use all sorts of swings: a high or a low backswing; a full, compact or short swing; a push; a pat; a flick; a horizontal, upwards or downwards movement through the impact point.

The important thing to remember is that the path of the racket head and racket face through the ball directs the shots.

With this knowledge and with mastery of the basic fundamentals of racket control outlined in this chapter, you can work out the most appropriate swing to get the best control of the shot you are playing.

Swing Size

The size of your squash swing depends on the pace and control you want. It is easier to hit softer with a short swing and harder with a fuller swing. Generally, the more compact a swing the more controlled it is. Don't try to use the same swing for every shot to disguise it. Disguise is a valid but special idea. Don't let it spoil getting the best control. Use the most appropriate swing for the shot.

There are a whole range of swings but two standard swings that can be practised and adapted for shots are the short swing and the full swing.

SHORT SWING

A short swing is often appropriate for drops, lobs and volleys.

On the forehand and backhand, start your backswing at waist height pointing your racket at the back wall. Use a firm wrist action in the swing and on the follow-through stop the racket head as it points at the front wall at waist height.

Practise this swing to develop a firm and controlled wrist action.

FULL SWING *(Figs 19 & 20)*

It may be easiest to think of the full swing as an extension of the compact swing.

Take the compact backswing back, around and up. Keep the racket clear of the body and overhead. On the follow-through push the elbow through as far as possible.

In the full swing, you want full movement around the shoulder and elbow. This full movement will generate more power in your shots.

25

| (a) | (b) | (c) |

| (d) | (e) | (f) |

Fig 19   The Full Swing: Forehand.

(a) Perfect preparation. A high steady backswing, with the shoulder and trunk turned. Jansher Khan is in an excellent position for the stroke to flow comfortably across his body. Note his concentration on the ball throughout this sequence.

(b) The front foot goes down and braces the body, the racket is about to come down with the elbow leading and the trunk has opened to the ball.

(c) The front knee bends and the weight transfers. The elbow and the butt lead the racket as the forearm is about to accelerate the racket head through the impact point. This turning action of the forearm is called pronation.

(d) The arm is straight at impact. Note the open racket face, the perfect balance, the concentration on the ball, the wrist up and the V grip.

(e) The swing comes through across the body. Note how Jansher holds himself steady as the racket swings through and how he is still concentrating on the impact zone.

(f) The racket swings through to a full follow-through with the wrist up and the racket head controlled. Note the swing has moved from a V to a V. His body is still balanced and not swinging with the shot. Jansher is already starting to push back.

(a)

(b)

(c)

(d)

(e)

(f)

Fig 20 The Full Swing: Backhand.
(a) Perfect preparation and positioning. The racket is overhead, the shoulder turned and the elbow right back behind the body. Jansher is about to stride into the shot, concentrating on the ball.
(b) Jansher's foot goes down and he braces himself to keep balance during the swing. The racket starts to go down and around the body. Note how the knees provide balance.
(c) The weight continues to move into the shot and the shoulder unwinds. The butt comes through first and the forearm starts to accelerate the racket through to impact. The forearm action is called supination.
(d) Jansher, steady throughout the stroke, concentrates on the impact area. The arm has straightened and the wrist is still up, giving good control over the racket head. Note the open racket face and the V grip.
(e) Note the perfect balance and control over the racket head as Jansher holds himself steady and swings through across his body.
(f) The swing has come right through in a smooth curve. Note Jansher still has good control of the racket head and is already pushing back from the shot.

Practise the full swing so that you can have power without sacrificing control.

Racket Speed

It is the speed of the racket head through the ball that gives the shot pace.

To hit it softly, the racket needs to move slowly and a short swing is best to 'time' this action. For pace, the full swing provides the best chance to develop racket head speed.

Practise to develop racket speed both from the speed and efficiency of your swing and the size of your swing.

Developing Your Swing

1. Study your technique and try to get it right to enable you to develop 'good' squash habits while practising, instead of ingraining faults.
2. Use the wobble, grip and feel checks to help you get the best grip and wrist action.
3. Practise your swing without the ball. Start with the *short* swing (for firm wrist movement), then progress to the *compact* swing (for developing forearm movement) and then to the *full* swing (for developing a full smooth path and movement from the shoulder).
   (a) Explore each point on the swing and check you have got things right.
   (b) Start with a slow, firm and careful action. Try to keep control and 'feel' of your racket head right through the swing.
   (c) Gradually build up speed. Stop and check yourself each time on the backswing and follow-through.
   (d) Repeat each swing at least ten times before going on to the next.

4. Practise your swing with the ball.

Take it slowly and endeavour to be aware of your racket as you practise.

Preparation and Timing

CONNECTION

The connection of the moving player with the moving racket and the moving ball is about 'time'. The novice tries to do everything at once, in a flash, he is moving and hitting in a very general way. Often, things go wrong and he only achieves a small percentage of shots that are controlled and feel right. He is surprised when he sees how much time top players have.

CREATE TIME FOR YOUR SHOTS

The expert tries to stop and control each aspect of the process. He tries to get in position early and be stopped and balanced for the shot. He takes his racket back as he moves so that when he arrives in position he is ready to hit the ball. In position, he pauses or gets a little 'stop' before he hits, waiting for the ball to get in exactly the right place. The expert performs this process quickly and precisely, but he takes time for his shot. Create time for your shots; this is where you get real control.

RACKET PREPARATION *(Fig 21)*

Beginners run to the ball before they start preparing. It often takes them longer to get the racket in position for the backswing than to swing through to impact How often have you run all the way to a difficult shot, got there and then missed it because your racket wasn't ready?

Racket preparation is a crucial part of your swing. It gets your racket quickly

Fig 21   Preparation. The striker beautifully balanced and prepared waits for the ball to get to just the right point before hitting.

and efficiently into the backswing position and helps create time for your shot.

From holding your racket directly in front of you, with your wrist up, take your racket head and edge directly back to the backswing position and hold it there. As you are moving for your shot, prepare your racket like this.

SEQUENCE

The sequence of good control and timing is watching, moving, preparing, positioning, stopping, hitting and recovering.

WATCHING THE BALL

This is the most basic requirement in timing 'the connection'. You would be surprised how often in the heat of battle, a player gets too close and moves backwards and looks up while hitting. Keep your head down on impact until you have finished your swing. Don't fall into the trap of looking up at the target area. This is a particular problem with the drop shot.

If you don't normally have trouble hitting the ball and you miss it, it is probably because you were not watching it.

PROBLEMS

Problems with hitting a ball can be caused by not watching and by poor technique, poor timing and poor ball control.

If you do have problems and you are watching, the best technique will give you the best chance of getting control. Use a short swing until you can hit it better. Don't try to hit too hard. Don't rush and mistime it.

If you haven't played a racket sport before, don't be discouraged if you aren't immediately successful. You will need lots of practice at developing 'hand to eye' co-ordination and developing correct technique. Use the ball control exercises daily. This will help.

AIMING *(Fig 22)*

To a large extent, you aim a squash ball by taking it in a particular place in relation to your body.

Imagine you are a fixed machine, with a mechanical arm totally grooved and you take the ball at precisely the same point each time. You then have control over the factors that affect the shot. As a firing machine, you could land the ball consistently on the dot.

If the moving player is stopped and stable, if the swing is grooved and if the ball is taken at the best point, then the shot can really be precise.

Fig 22 Former World Champion, Rodney Martin, one of the game's great shot makers, lines the ball up.

'Lining the ball up' – being in the best position, having your racket ready and waiting for the ball to get to the point where you want to hit it, I call 'lining the ball up'. We could call it just as easily 'setting the shot up'. This is where you get complete accuracy and where you can play down the 'line of the shot'.

FAULTS

All sorts of things can spoil your movement control, your racket control and your timing. Without control over these, your aiming will be inaccurate and your placement inconsistent.

Space won't permit me to point out everything that can go wrong with your shots but it is useful to look at some of the common problems so you can recognize them (in yourself and others) and attempt to remedy them.

A fault that has become a bad habit may be limiting your game and may take great effort and some time to correct. The rewards, however, may be a developing game rather than one that is on a plateau.

COURT MOVEMENT (Fig 23)

Getting to the ball, or more correctly, getting into position (the place where you want to hit the ball from) is vital to your success as a squash player. Obviously, you cannot hit the ball if you don't get there. Half the game is getting in the right place to hit the ball. If you are correctly positioned, balanced and have your racket ready, all that remains to do is to swing your racket through when the ball is at the right point. All the important work is done before you actually connect with the ball.

Why don't you always get to the ball? Is it really because you lack fitness? Do you really not have enough time? Are your tactics creating the time you need? Are you slow taking off or just slow? Do you run too far? Do you read the game badly? Could just improving your movement habits improve your squash?

Observe players in your club. Work out why they don't always get to a particular ball. Is it fitness? Are they slow? Or is it problems like poor recovery, not watching, not being ready to move off, being on their heels, poor tactics, not reading opponents' shots, front wall watching, running in circles and uncontrolled movement?

30

Fig 23   Movement: at speed and under pressure the striker although airborne has already started to the swing. Note the total focus on the ball.

Of course, fitness is important. It is often crucial. It may prove you a winner at your level or help you move up a level, but it is not the whole story.

Speed is important but the vital part of being fast around a squash court is not how fast you move but when you move and where you move from. To give yourself the best chance to get to the ball, move as soon as you know where it is going.

Several points follow. You should watch your opponent and the ball. Be ready to move off quickly, and after hitting the ball recover to the T so you can repeat the sequence and hence get to the next ball. The key to good recovery is to be back in position before your opponent hits the ball.

Court movement like racket control and movement control is not just about ability, it is also about having good squash habits. These are the things you can work at and get better at: they include watching, the ready position, recovery and the paths and positioning. Let's look at them in turn.

Watching

Watch the ball and your opponent. Follow the ball with your eyes. Try to see the ball come off your opponent's racket. Watch his footwork, positioning, and backswing for hints as to the direction of the shot. To anticipate, don't race off before you see the ball, but be ready to move.

Study your opponent's play. Observe the range of shots he uses from certain situations and work out your counter moves before you need them. Be aware of the ball in relation to his body position and the walls. Perhaps he has a wide range of alternatives and you should cover them all from the T, or perhaps he is limited to one or two options and you can calculate the move in and narrow the angle and distance.

For example, a ball that passed your opponent and won't come off the back wall enough for a crosscourt shot will limit your opponent to a straight drive or boast. This will allow you to move in and intercept perhaps with a volley boast while still covering his option to boast.

Angle your shots into the side walls so your opponent cannot crosscourt then move in to volley.

FAULT FINDING

Faults	Problems
Rushing	Off balance, moving while hitting, mistiming, inaccuracy, inconsistent shots.
Moving while hitting	Inaccurate and inconsistent shots. Difficulty recovering after shot.
Swinging your body	Inaccurate and inconsistent shots. Moving your head and taking your eye off the ball. Pulling the shot around.
Too close	Cramped. No room for a full swing. Leaning back while hitting. Head coming up, eye off ball. Too upright. No transfer of weight.
Too upright (not bending knees)	Poor balance. Difficulty braking. Poor transfer of weight. Not getting down to the ball.
Poor positioning	Poor balance, excess body movement. Often compensated for with a less accurate, wristy shot.
Too large or wild swinging Excess follow-through Uncontrolled swing	Missing, mistiming, loss of touch. Less control and consistency. Dangerous. Difficulty in corners and close to wall. Often necessary to rush shot. Hitting down on ball. Difficulty in reacting quickly.
Poor racket preparation	Rushing, missing, mistiming, a less grooved swing.
Poor preparation	No time to line the ball up.
Loose/dropped wrist	Weak link, less racket head control. Inconsistent swing.
Rolled wrist Closed racket face Grip slips	Ball goes low or down. Drop shots into tin. Poor lobs and back corner shots. Missed or uncontrolled shots.
Eye off ball	Missing.

Solutions

Stop for your shot. Use the stop and freeze techniques in solo practice. Wait until the ball comes to you. Try walking. Develop good racket preparation. Create the time you need. Vary the pace. Recover to a ready position on the T. Play tighter shots. Watch your opponent.

Practise slowly concentrating on balance. Use the stop, freeze and push checks. Check your positioning. Use your knees to brake.

Check positioning. Stop and stay on balance for your shot. Practise straight driving and hold your shoulders facing the side.

Check positioning. Prepare early and stop. Wait for the ball to come to you. Reach out for your shot. Use your knees. Move up and down the middle, keeping your feet out of the service box width. Practise straight drives keeping your feet outside service box width. Try to keep out of this area in a game. Use the pairs practice, boasting and driving. Move away from a ball that comes at you.

Leave room between yourself and the ball (see above). Use knees. Practise stances. Do some footwork and stretching exercises.

Don't run for the ball. Do move to the place you want to hit the ball from. This is positioning. Use solo and pairs practices and concentrate on positioning.

Use a swing that is appropriate to your level of skill. Use a compact swing when learning. Practise without ball, with ball, a compact swing, quick reflex drives, reflex volleys. Don't sacrifice control for pace. Start your backswing lower. Swing through the ball.

Don't wait until the ball has bounced before you move your racket. Prepare your racket as you move. When practising, take the racket back when the ball hits the front wall.

Get into position early and wait until the ball is just in the right place before you hit it.

Keep wrist up throughout the swing. Use the feel check. Practise without the ball and with the ball. Use a short swing.

Use grip and feel checks. Don't let the grip creep around and close the racket face. Practise hitting through and up on the ball. Use V- grip and checks. Hold the grip firmly but not too tightly. Check the grip every time play stops. Change racket grip regularly. Use a grip aid.

Keep watching until you have finished your swing. Freeze and check you are still looking at impact point after shot.

Ready Position *(Fig 24)*

The place that will give you the best opportunity of covering the whole court, that is the four corners, will be between the short line (the line across the court that is short of half-way) and the imaginary line joining the back of the service boxes.

Players generally lag too far back. You must at least get over this imaginary line and preferably about a racket's length behind the short line. This position is called 'on the T'.

Crouch with knees bent, putting your weight forward like a sprinter, so you are 'on your toes' and ready to move quickly.

Try this. Now, rock back on your heels. This is a position you should never get into in your game.

Place your feet either side of the half-court line and your toes to the front. From here, you will be centrally positioned and be able to move off in either direction. If you have your toes and body facing the side or back you may be caught out and have to waste valuable time in turning before you can move to the ball.

Sit your racket up in front (i.e. pointing at the front wall) with your wrist up. From here, it is ready to move for both the forehand and backhand.

Turn your head and shoulders to watch your opponent and the ball.

Fig 24   Ready Position: the striker is prepared and about to move into his back corner stance while his opponent crouches astride the T in a ready position and watches.

JUMP

Many top players use a fast, small astride jump that puts their feet wide so that they can push off powerfully from either foot. Watch their feet. Can you see it?

Recovery

To cover your opponent's shots, you need to be on the T, in a ready position and watching. The overall success of your court coverage depends on your ability to continually sustain this sequence. It depends on how well you recover.

Immediately you have finished your stroke, push back and recover the T quickly. Don't, however, pull away as you are hitting and spoil your shot and don't rush back so quickly that it is impossible to change direction.

From the front of the court, push back from the bent knee position and as you back pedal to the T keep your weight forward so that you could push off forward again if necessary. Turn your head and shoulders and watch the ball as you move.

From the back of the court, you can often walk briskly back to the T. Try to turn from the back court stance and step with the foot nearest the middle back towards the half-court line allowing room for your opponent to move into the corner.

From the side push back from the bent knee position and sidestep back.

You can only stop twice in a squash rally. Stop for your shot and stop when you have recovered the T.

Paths and Positioning *(Fig 25)*

Remember, don't run to the ball, move to the place you want to hit the ball from.

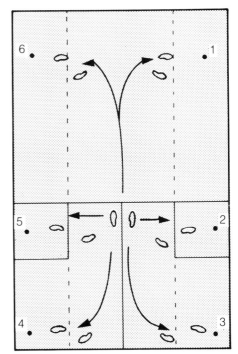

Fig 25   Paths and stations: (a) Move up and down the middle. (b) Try to keep outside the 'sidelines'. (c) Move directly to a spot one step away from your position. (d) Don't run to the ball, move to the place you want to hit it from.

In squash, you are continually calculating where to move to. As soon as you see the ball, calculate where it will travel to, which point will be the best place to hit it at (impact) and which point to hit it from (position). The shortest route to this position is your path.

The path you take is generally more up and down the middle of the court (and outside the sidelines) than directly at the ball. This is because you must leave room between your position and the ball, room to step into your position and a path that will allow you to cover both sides of the court if your decision is wrong.

35

Place a ball on the court floor. Work out the position you want to hit it from and then the path from your ready position. This is shadow practice. Let's look at the speed and efficiency of the movement you use on this path.

Movement

When Jonah Barrington (six times winner of the British Open title) paid tribute to his old rival, the great Geoff Hunt (eight times winner of the title), of all the things he could have said about Hunt's abilities, one stood out. 'There never was, nor ever will be, a better balanced mover on court and, in these last years, as perfectly oiled a machine so capable of producing the goods with such simple efficiency.'

The six times World Open Champion, Jansher Khan, smooth and economical, glides around the court effortlessly, walking quickly as much as he can. When required he dives, racket outstretched, and then cat like collects his feet under him before pushing back. Even when caught out of position in the front court he quickly slips into a ready position and with lightning reflexes from this narrowed angle he often snaps away an intercept winner.

Jahangir Khan, ten times the British Open Champion, was smooth and powerful, frequently turning his shoulder as he moved to wind up like a spring and then unwind powerfully. From the back court, he often hit the ball off the back foot but with his body well positioned and beautifully balanced.

Rarely do you see top players collapse in a heap and push off the walls. Qamar Zaman was a dancer on court, you could not even hear him on the boards.

Squash movement is an individual thing. We run, walk, sidestep, lunge, jump, skip, use crossovers, adjusting steps, shuffles, swivels, bounces, backward runs and quick foot changes. Training for squash movement should involve practice in all these so they can be performed smoothly and efficiently.

Next time you get the chance to watch some top squash players, forget the ball for a while, watch the players' feet, their movements and the path they take to the ball.

Work on your movement. Move early, quickly, economically and smoothly.

MOVE EARLY

Watch, study, use the ready position from the T and move as soon as you know where the ball is going.

MOVE ECONOMICALLY

In shadow practice and in your game, work out the steps you need and keep them to a comfortable minimum. Eliminate unnecessary steps. Adjust the size of your steps so you arrive in just the right place. Use sidesteps and sliding steps to adjust when you have to. You shouldn't need more than one adjusting step.

TURNING

First, step and point your toe in the direction you want to move on the foot nearest that direction. Turn the hips in this direction. Turn or swivel and step through on the back foot. Don't swing your body and shoulders to turn and change direction moving in a wide circle. Try to turn using only one turning step.

CHANGING DIRECTION

The real efficiency of a player's movement is seen when they are under pressure and when they have to change direction. Move in such a way that you can still change direction. Move so that you are balanced and controlled. Try to give your movement the advantage of your ready position which allows you to move in any direction. All sorts of things are happening in a game of squash and it is not the best place to develop your movement or sort out your movement habits. Here are some ideas on improving them.

PRACTISING COURT MOVEMENT

Shadow Practice

Work out your movement problems without the ball using shadow practice. Take time to work out the path, position and movement you will use for a particular ball before you put it under pressure. Practise slowly, get the steps right, then use your racket and co-ordinate this with the movement in the stroke. Move a marker ball to various parts of the court. Work on one shot at a time then put them together.

Shadow Training

Shadow training incorporates shuttle running and shadow practice.

1. *Front corners* From a ready position, run forward to the forehand corner preparing your racket and play a forehand straight drive. Recover backwards to the T. Repeat on the backhand side. Continue, alternating corners.
2. *Back corners* From a ready position, step back and turn your right foot towards the back corner. Run or jump into the corner to land in a squat posi-

tion. To recover, step back towards the T on the left foot and walk briskly. Repeat on the other side.
3. *Four corners* The above two exercises together.
4. *Turning*
   (a) *Ready position* Start in a ready position.
   (b) *Turning step* Step and point your toe to the side on the right foot.
   (c) *Step* Step across your body on the left and as you do, prepare your racket. Swing after your foot has gone down. Swivel comfortably on the ball of the back foot.
   (d) *Recover and turn* Push back off your left foot, swivel on the right and point the left foot at the side.
   (e) *Step* Step, prepare, stop, stroke.
   (f) *Recover* Recover and repeat.
5. *Lunging* As with the above exercise, but using a longer turning step and a lunge (or a jumping lunge). This will cover more ground but prove more difficult to push back from.
6. *Sidesteps and lunging* Use the full width of the court and several sidesteps between each lunge.

Ghosting

Ghosting is shadow practice under pressure. This is a timed pressure session. For training times, turn to the fitness section. An example may be six to ten sets of 45 seconds exercise with 30 seconds rest.

1. *Random ghosting* Ghosting can be done to imaginary points but I tend to prefer the player to have specific stations to reach so he has to adjust his movement to a definite point.
2. *Stations* Start from a ready position and run to each of the stations in turn,

37

recovering to a ready position each time. Try to keep the quality of your movement and see how many you can do in a minute.

Place the squash balls or half squash balls on the floor so you have a specific impact point. Start with six stations then progress to twelve.

3. *Numbers and signs* When working with a partner, he can stand at the front wall and call the number of the station you are to proceed to next. He can do this before you have recovered to the T, thus introducing change of direction into the exercise. Alternatively, he could just point to a station forcing the moving player to keep his eyes on him.

Squash Movement Practices

SQUASH SOLO MOVEMENT PRACTICES

Three very good solo movement practices outlined in the practice section are front court boasting, the corner exercise and the double corner exercise.

How many continuous boasts can you do that hit the floor then the opposite side? Try six sets of thirty, building to six sets of fifty.

SQUASH PAIRS MOVEMENT PRACTICE

In your pairs practice you have a good chance to work on your shots and your movement.

An excellent practice is to boast and drive which will allow you to get into a smooth rhythm on your movement and your shots. We will cover this in the pairs practice section.

COACHING MOVEMENT EXERCISES

Working with a coach is the ideal situation. He will be able to instruct you on the best movement and design exercises for your individual needs.

PRACTISING TECHNIQUE

We have looked at the elements of technique and used checks and practices on the swing, stance and court movement.

Grooving the whole stroke can be practised without the ball (as a golfer does). Now we can put the various parts together into a sequence. Use this chapter as reference when you wish to check points. Progress slowly. Stop and check at each count (you may also wish to stop at impact) and gradually build up speed until you have a smooth and grooved action. Count the number or positions aloud as you go.

Stroking Sequence (without ball)
(Figs 26 & 27)

1. Ready position.
   Check – Feet level, weight forward on balls of feet, knees slightly bent, racket in front, racket face vertical, wrist up.
2. Step.
   Check – Step to a basic stance and point your toe at the side wall. As you step, turn your upper body, take your shoulder around and take your racket (racket head first) to the backswing position. Attempt to have your racket back and body around before your foot hits the floor.
3. Pause.
   Check – Pause and check. Pause to assist timing. Everything is ready. Wait for the ball and...
4. Swing.
   Check – Use a smooth swing. Use the feel check on the follow-through.

5. Recover.

Check – When you have completely finished the swing, push back with one movement to the ready position.

Count each number and stage aloud as you go through them, and then repeat the exercise.

(a)

(b)

(c)

(d)

Fig 26 Stroking Sequence: Forehand.
(a) Ready Position. (b) Step and pause.
(c) Impact. (d) Follow-through.

Technique Practices (with ball)

If we take the pat exercise we used in the ball control section and turn it into a 'side on' stroke, we have the makings of a squash shot. Use a basic stance (rather than an upright one) and a side-arm action (rather than an underarm one) with a cocked wrist.

Slowly Start these exercises slowly, concentrating on swing, racket preparation, wrist action, positioning, footwork, distance from the ball, using your knees, stopping for your shot.

Check Stop regularly and check your swing and stance.

Concentrate Work on one idea at a time. Concentrate on it, get it right and then move on and pick up another idea. Remember to come back and re-check.

Short drives Use a short swing and practise softly in front of the short line. Aim above the cut.

Service box drives Use a compact swing and practise into the service box.

Technique Progression

Once you have control, you can gradually increase the pace of the drives using this progression.

39

(a)

(b)

(c)

(d)

Fig 27 Stroking Sequence: Backhand.
(a) Ready Position. (b) Step and pause. (c) Impact. (d) Follow-through.

could break down under pressure. Gradually progress to this point.

HIGH DRIVES
From behind the service box, continuously lift the ball to just under the out of court line.

LENGTH DRIVES
Throw the ball off the back wall and using a full swing, aim the ball just above the cut line to bounce and rebound off the back. Do this continuously. Occasionally, to keep the practice continuous, you may have to take the ball before the back and let it bounce twice where necessary. Use a faster ball (e.g. blue or red dot) if this will help you get into a rhythm.

Technique Sequences

1. Short swing – without ball – 10.
   Short drives – with ball – 2 mins.
   Compact swing – without ball – 10.
   Service box drives above cut line – 5 to 10 mins.
   (Concentrate on one side first, e.g. forehand, and then move to the other. For example 10 mins on forehand then the same on the backhand or concentrate on the weakness.)

1. Service box drives all above the cut line.
2. One above and one below the cut line.
3. All below the cut line.
4. Reflex drives in front of the short line and quite hard.

This is where your control and technique

2. Service box drives using technique progression.
3. Number 1 or 2 followed by high drives and length drives.

TECHNIQUE SUMMARY

1. Good technique gives you accuracy and consistency in your shots.
2. To get good control over a squash ball you need control over your movement, your racket and to 'time' the connection with the ball.
3. Test your percentage ball control.
4. Movement control means correct positioning, distance from the ball, footwork and balance.
5. Don't run to the ball. Do move to the place you want to hit it from.
6. Use the freeze check.
7. Racket control means correct grip, wrist and swing.
8. 'Feel' your racket head. Use the checks: grip, wobble and feel.
9. Use different size swings: short, compact and full.
10. Take time for your shots.
11. Use racket preparation.
12. Line the ball up.
13. Try to eliminate faults.
14. Develop good court movement habits: watching, ready position and recovery.
15. Move, take off, turn and change direction economically. Practise using the shadow practices.
16. Use the 'stroking sequence' to practise your technique at home.
17. Make time to practise your technique. Use the technique sequences.

2
Basic Shots

Squash is a combative game. Shots are the weapons we use. Our success depends on their consistency and accuracy. Master your basic armoury well before you go to war.

PLACEMENT *(Figs 28–30)*

When you have good control over your technique you will be able to place the ball consistently. With alterations in the way you line it up you will be able to control its placement and become accurate.

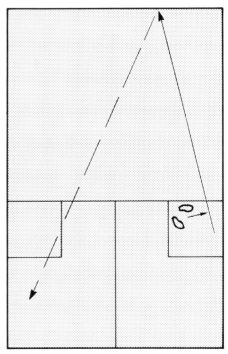

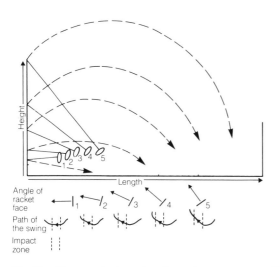

Fig 28   The vertical angle of service. The height of your stroke affects the length. Hit higher to get more length. These strokes are played at approximately the same pace. The vertical angle is determined by the angle of the racket face and the path of the swing.

Fig 29   The horizontal angle of service: wrong – ball returns too near the centre as positioning is too far around the other side.

To have your shots 'grooved' is to be accurate and consistent.

The alterations that control the placement of your shots are the horizontal and vertical angles. The line of the shot is at right angles to the direction the body faces. Changing the horizontal angle of your shot is just a matter of changing your positioning in relation to the ball. Changing the vertical angle of your shot is achieved by changing the angle of the racket face and the path of the swing. With control over both of these angles, you can place the ball exactly where you want.

When you practise, think in terms of angles. Talk to yourself, 'Up a bit; over more; back a bit.'

The horizontal angle affects how wide the shot goes. The vertical angle affects how high and long it goes. For example:

1. If your serve is not hitting the side you will need to angle it across the front wall a little more. You could do this by positioning slightly around to the front.

2. If your serve is not going deep enough you will have to hit it higher. Alter the path of your swing and the face of your racket to get under the ball and lift it higher on to the front wall.

Target Areas

Ask a beginner where they have trouble getting the ball, and they will reply, high at the side wall on return of serve and out of the back corners. They may add when it is tight to the side and in the front corners.

The best area to 'place' a squash ball is where your opponent has most trouble getting to it (in the corners) and most difficulty hitting it (tight, clinging, dying, dead).

CORNERS
Use the extremities of the court. Make your opponent move as far as possible.

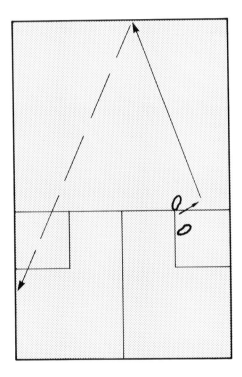

Aspects of Placement

LENGTH
A ball that bounces in the back and forces your opponent to take it off the back wall is a 'full' length.

A ball that bounces in the back and would not die on the back wall (i.e. not bounce out) forcing an opponent to get it before the back is a 'dying' length.

Fig 30   Right – a change of positioning allows the correct angle and good width.

WIDTH

A 'good' width is where the ball is on the side wall at the point your opponent would want to hit it.

A 'dying' width is a shot whose second bounce dies on the side.

HEIGHT

One of the simplest and most crucial ideas in squash is to be able to use the height of the front wall. Hit the ball high to get it in the back corners. Master this simple idea, practise it. It is the key to your success as a player. Use the height of your shot to go over a player as well as width to go around him.

TIGHT

A ball or rally close to the side that gives no chance of an easy intercept.

CLINGER

A shot that is moved into the side and rolls along it.

NICK

A shot that is aimed to come off the front and hit the joint between the wall and the floor. A 'dead' nick will roll.

DYING

Bouncing for the second time.

LOOSE

A shot that has come a long way out from the sides presenting an opportunity to attack.

SHORT

A shot aimed down the court that has landed too short to be a length shot (i.e. in the middle).

DEFENSIVE SHOTS

Straight Drive *(Figs 31–37)*

Squash is a hard driving game. How well you cover the court and how well you drive sets your standard as a player.

There is room for all sorts of players: power players, shot players, volleyers, tough players, lob and drop merchants,

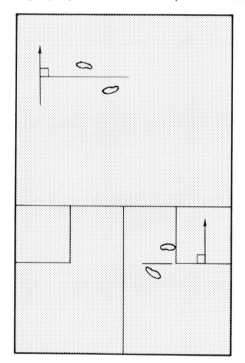

Fig 31   Straight drive: position – face the side wall and keep the ball between yourself and the side.

Fig 32   (right) Straight drive: path – don't run to the ball. Move to the side of it.

Fig 33   (far right) Straight drive: placement – angle the ball slightly so it will move in towards the side and touch behind the service box. This is good width.

Fig 34   Former World Champion, Ross Norman, strokes the ball down the straight alleyway. The closed stance has faced his body to the side wall and it has only turned a little with the swing. Note how he is already pushing back from the shot while finishing the follow-through.

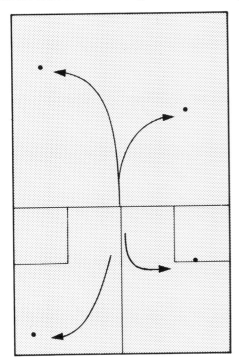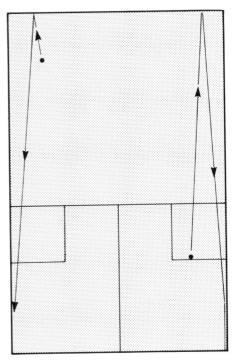

45

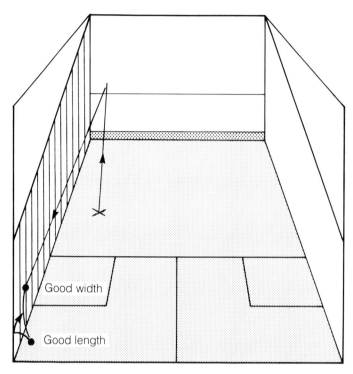

Fig 35   Straight drive: placement – aim high enough to make the ball bounce and come off the back. This is good length.

tricky players (you may have run into one or two) – but they must all drive.

You may display the most amazing wizardry on the drop or have a sensational volley nick, but your standard is set by how accurately, consistently and powerfully you drive.

Driving is the foundation of your game. Jahangir Khan built his game on relentless driving at such a pace that his opponents failed to handle the pressure.

Don't, however, sacrifice accuracy and consistency for pace. Don't become a basher. Line the ball up and place it. Hold on to this accuracy and gradually build up the pace. Jansher Khan rolls the ball down the walls to immaculate length and then

picks his moment to attack or pressurize his opponent.

OBJECTIVES
1. A good length drive will force your opponent out of position and give you time to take control of the T.
2. The first requirement is safety. Play a 'tight' shot that does not give your opponent a chance to attack.
3. Try to force a weak ball.
4. Try to force a mistake.

TARGET AREA
Drive for full length and good width. Aim to hit the side wall behind the service box before or after hitting the back.

The straight drive is the tightest shot in squash. It keeps tight to the side wall for its full path.

METHOD
Guided Forehand
1. Position yourself facing the side in a basic stance with your front foot on the 'sideline', pointing directly at the side four inches (10cm) forward of the back of the box.
2. Point your back toe to the back corner.
3. Point your racket at the back wall at shoulder height and swing down and up. Stop your racket at the front wall. Practise this.
4. Prepare your racket.
5. Throw the ball high off the side to land half-way out on the back line of the service box.

(a)   (b)   (c)

Fig 36   Forehand straight drive. (a) Note position and racket preparation. (b) Impact is where the racket makes a right angle with the side wall. Note the stance, transfer of weight, distance from the ball, cocked wrist, open racket face and the eyes on the ball. (c) Follow-through to the front wall. Note how the body is steady and balanced and that the swing has been across the body.

(a)   (b)   (c)

Fig 37   Backhand straight drive. (a) As the shoulder is in front of the body on the backhand, the impact point is further forward and your position is further behind the service box. Point your backswing directly at the back wall. (b) Impact. Make a right angle with the side wall. (c) Follow-through. Point your racket directly at the front wall.

6. Stroke under the ball and lift it above the cut line.
7. Skill. How many single shots can you play out of ten to land in the area behind the service box?
8. Practise. Start as above and lift the ball into the service box, adjust your feet for the next shot and practise continuously.

Backhand
1. Position at side and six inches (15cm) behind the box.

Numbers 2 to 8 as above.

47

GENERAL

Endeavour to to keep your body steady and your shoulders parallel with the side throughout the shot.

Impact is where your racket makes a right angle with the side wall. To angle your ball in for good width let it come back a little past the right angle. This angle will be greater the further out from the side you are. You never hit the ball closer to the front than a right angle.

Position yourself so the ball is between you and the side wall. The path you take should always put you in this position.

IMPACT POINT

The impact point on the forehand will be just behind the knee. The impact point on the backhand will be forward of the knee.

VARIATIONS

Vary your length between full length and dying length depending on your opponent's position and the time you need to recover the T.

Vary the height and pace of your shots to create the time you need or to apply pressure. You have a full range of shots using the complete height of the wall. Keep the ball below the out of court line along its full path so as not to take the risk of hitting out.

PRACTICE

Use the technique practices to the service box to groove drives.

To practise length, solo drive continuously from the back corners (consider using a fast ball) and use the pairs practice where player A front court drops and drives and player B backcourt drives straight and boasts; and the circling practice.

Crosscourt Drive *(Figs 38–41)*

The crosscourt drive is a dangerous shot. There are both risks and rewards.

It is dangerous because it spends a large part of its time out from the side wall and tends to be 'loose'. It risks being intercepted and hence leaving you out of position. Beginners tend to run to the ball, play it in front of them and hit a lot of loose crosscourts. Better players play more straight drives and pick their crosscourts.

Do not play crosscourts when your opponent is right up on the T, as it is easier for him to intercept here. Tend to play more straight drives than crosscourts from the back of the court.

Crosscourt from the middle and front and especially when your opponent is back in the court a little. This gives you

Fig 38   Ross Norman prepares for a backhand crosscourt. Note how the toe is forward to the corner and the ball is sitting out in front in the crosscourt position.

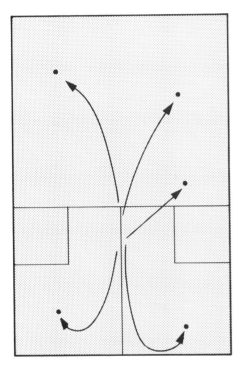

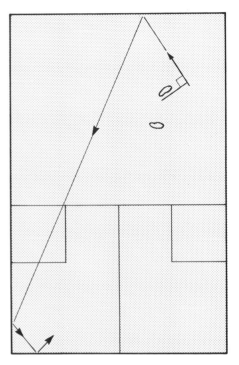

Fig 39 Crosscourt drive: paths – move so as to keep the ball slightly in front of your position. Hit smoothly across your body for good width.

Fig 40 Crosscourt drive: position and placement – target crosscourts to hit the side, floor and back.

(a)   (b)   (c)

Fig 41 Forehand crosscourt drive. (a) Backswing – toe pointing at the front corner, racket pointing at the back corner. (b) Impact is out in front of the body. (c) Follow-through is across the body and to the front left corner.

more chance of beating his volley by getting the ball into the side.

The rewards of a good crosscourt are that the ball comes across the court in the back rather than rebounding totally to the front as with the straight drive. This keeps the ball closer into the back and it proves difficult to return.

OBJECTIVES
1. To beat your opponent with good width.
2. Force him into a corner.
3. Force a weak boast which you can attack.
4. Give yourself more time, i.e. the crosscourt has a longer path.
5. There is more chance of hitting a nick or dying length than on a straight drive.

TARGET AREA – SIDE, FLOOR, BACK
Play the crosscourt to hit the side wall behind the service box (about half-way to the back), bounce on the floor and just drop off the back wall. This is good width and a full length. You do not want the ball to sit up off the back and give your opponent the option of a crosscourt. Limit him to a boast or a straight drive.

A hard 'low' dying length crosscourt will be aimed for the nick or floor behind the service box. A medium pace drive is aimed low on the side and a high crosscourt is wider and higher on the side. If your opponent is forward looking for the intercept and you are forced to crosscourt, play the ball into the side wall in front of him beating the volley.

METHOD
Guided Forehand
1. Position yourself half-way between the T and service box.
2. Step forward into a basic stance and point your toe at the front corner.

3. Point your back toe to the side.
4. Point your racket at shoulder height at the back corner and swing through to the opposite back corner.
5. Prepare your racket, drop the ball and swing under and up on the ball.
6. Endeavour to hit the side wall behind the service box, the floor and then the back.
7. Skill. Play ten shots. How many can you get to hit the side, floor, back?

Backhand
1. Step towards the corner and slightly move to the side.
2. Drop the ball slightly in front of the line between your front foot and the side near the corner.

GENERAL
Do not swing your body, turn or flick the ball to get it across.

Position yourself so the ball is between you and the corner. The path is more directly to the ball than the straight drive, but is still via the centre. Ideally you would position yourself so you had the option of taking the ball forward for the crosscourt or at the side for the straight drive.

The stroke is really the same as the straight drive, your position has just turned from the side to the corner so you can take the ball further out in front.

When crosscourting from the back corner, make sure that the ball has come out enough past your body so you can get an angle right across the side wall without playing a weak flick.

VARIATIONS
Again you have the whole height of the front wall to play with and can vary the height, pace, length and width of your shots.

PRACTICE

The best pairs exercise for crosscourts is boast and crosscourt.

Lob *(Figs 42 & 43)*

The lob is the most underrated and underused shot in squash. It is a shot for the artist. It hangs in the air and falls almost vertically to die in the back corners.

Use the lob to create time when you are under pressure (it may take five times as long before your opponent plays it as a hard low drive). Use it to vary the pace of a rally and to change the pace of a game. Slow the game if you are tired or

temporarily in oxygen debt. Use the lob if your opponent is weak or has lost confidence in the air.

OBJECTIVES
1. Lob when under pressure to create time, so you can recover the T.
2. Lob to vary the pace of a rally, slow a game and attack a weak volley.
3. Lob with a cold ball and get it to die in the back.

TARGET AREA – SIDE, FLOOR, BACK
1. Play the lob high and wide crosscourt to hit the side wall high up behind the service box. Keep it at least two feet (61cm) from the out of court line so you have a reasonable margin for error in your shots.
2. A very high lob will be more towards the back corner (beating an opponent with height).
3. A lower lob will be wider.

METHOD
1. Bounce the ball on your racket, hitting it straight up in the air. When you lob you want your racket to come down under the ball and up on it like this.

Guided Forehand and Backhand
2. Stand half-way between the short line and the front, and the half-court line and the side.
3. Position yourself so that the 'line' between your feet points at the corner. Use a squat stance, so you can get under the ball easily.

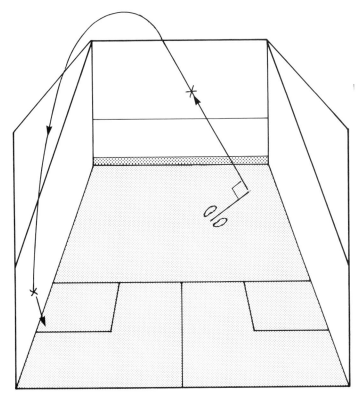

Fig 42 Lob: get down under the ball and lift it high so it will fall and hit the side wall behind the service box.

Fig 43   The lob: Ross Norman in an open stance with the racket low and about to come up under the ball. Note the open racket face.

4. Drop the ball on this line.
5 Start your backswing low as in the short swing. Use a firm wrist and an open racket face.
6. Stroke smoothly down, under and up on the ball. Get a sharp angle and endeavour to get the ball high up on the front wall.
7. Practice. Throw some balls above the cut line to land between you and the front wall. Practise lobbing.
8. Skill. Throw ten balls. How many can you get to hit the side and land behind the service box?

GENERAL

When under pressure you will, of course, have to lunge.

The quickest way and best reach for a forehand lob is off the 'wrong' foot. This open stance proves a useful position for the crosscourt lob, but on the straight lob endeavour to use the classic forehand footwork and position, a short swing and keep the ball below the out of court line.

VARIATIONS

There are several variations of height and width. The high lob will fall down into the back corner. The semi-lob will be wider, placed to beat the volley and die. The narrow or cling lob is played to hit the back wall first, hit the floor and move into the side.

PRACTICE

Boast and lob (see pairs practice), also volley boast and lob.

SERVICE (Figs 44–46)

One of the little things you notice about playing Jonah Barrington is how much time and care he takes on his serve and how difficult it is to get back.

Unfortunately at club level the serve is often wasted with a poor and hurried shot. Take all the time and care you need. It is the one shot you can hit exactly as you want. Do not spoil it by rushing. Get the best serve you can and get on top right at the start of the rally.

Use this time to compose yourself mentally and tactically.

RULES

1. To be 'good', a service must go above the cut (service) line and land within the lines of the opposite back quarter of the court. If on or below the cut line or outside the quarter it is a 'fault'.
2. The server must have at least one foot completely inside the service box. If not

it is a fault and is called a 'foot fault'.
3. If the ball is served out, below the tin, missed or hits a side wall first it is a handout or service change.

OBJECTIVES
1. To get the ball safely into play (so it cannot be attacked).
2. Provide a problem for the receiver by forcing him to place a weak ball or make a mistake.
3. Put the server in control of the T and the receiver out of position.

TARGET AREA – SIDE, FLOOR, BACK
Generally high into the side wall behind or about the back of the service box.

METHOD: SEMI-LOB SERVICE – RIGHT SIDE
1. Put the heel of your left foot on the intersection of the short and 'side-lines' and point it towards the front corner. The right foot will be approximately four inches (10cm) inside the box and 1ft behind the short line. The toe points at the side.
2. Stand facing the corner with the weight evenly balanced on each foot. When serving take a small step or let the weight move forward onto the front foot.
3. Use a short swing. Start the back-swing at waist height and pointing at the back corner, racket face open.
4. Hold the ball, palm up, out between the feet and one foot forward of the line. Use a small throw about six inches (15cm) high.
5. Swing with a firm wrist down under and up through the ball. Use a short follow-through.
6. Lift the ball up between the lines and onto the side wall. Imagine the half-court line extended up the front wall.

Fig 44   The Serve: Jahangir Khan prepares to serve from the right box. He uses a low racket angle and an open racket face to lift the ball onto the front wall. Note how his weight will rock from the right foot to the left so that he can move quickly to the T.

Aim your service approximately 2ft (61cm) to the right of this line.

Vary the angle back and forth along the wall (by small alterations in your positioning if necessary) until you get the correct width. Vary the height and pace to get the desired length. Allow a margin for error between your target area and the out of court line on the side wall. Do not aim an inch below the line, or you may end up hitting out.
7. Move to the ready position on the T and anticipate the return. Look for the intercept.
8. Skill. Serve ten times. How many can you get to hit the side, floor and back?

Fig 45   The semi-lob from the right box.

Fig 46   The service follow-through with the weight through onto the left foot.

METHOD: SEMI-LOB SERVICE – LEFT SIDE

1. Stand at the front of the box and step on the left foot along the short line. Keep the right foot in the box, and the toe pointing at the right back corner.
2. As you hit, step along the short line.
3. Hold the ball palm up out over the line.
4. Aim about 3ft (1m) to the right of the extended half-court line. As the impact point is quite near the T you actually aim further to the right than on the right box service, The angle of this serve is narrower and it is therefore easier to hit out. A slightly lower and firmer service will be safest.
5. Serve, take up a ready position on the T and look for the intercept.
6. Skill. Serve ten times. How many can you get to hit the side floor and back?

TYPES OF SERVICE

Lob Very high and soft, just below the out of court line. Use an open racket face and underarm action. Use a narrower angle for safety. Can be risky.

Semi-lob Standard service using a side-on action.

Low Fairly safe. A harder, safer service just above the cut line and firmly into the side.

Smash A hard service using a smash or tennis service type action (overarm), and aimed for the side wall nick behind the service box, the back wall nick or the floor so it hits the back and comes in to 'cling'.

Backhand From the right box only. Provides a good view of the receiver and easy access to T. A narrow angle stays closer to the wall.

Bodyline This is my favourite – save it for the right moment. A soft service to 'die', or a hard service to 'rattle', aimed straight at the receiver's body. Best angled into an opponent's right shoulder when serving from the right, providing a difficult choice as to which way to move. The soft one does not come off the back and may force a boast.

Corkscrew See Chapter 3.

PRACTICE

The service is easy to practise solo. Ten shots may be enough as the ball will cool. Warm the ball with another exercise and repeat.

Practise serving and returning with a partner.

Return of Service *(Figs 47 & 48)*

Many a game has faulted on a flimsy return of service. This is a defensive situation. You can lose points. The main requirement is to return the ball and return it safely. There may be occasional opportunities to attack but overall emphasis is on defence. Try to get your opponent off the T, put him deep and win control of the T position for yourself.

STANDARD RETURN

The standard return of service is the straight drive or volley down the side wall. This is the shot you should look for in most cases.

Occasionally you will choose or be forced to play a crosscourt. Try to use this variation sparingly as a loose crosscourt will provide your opponent with opportunities in the air.

TARGET AREAS

1. On the straight return aim for good length and width. Endeavour to angle the ball into the side so it cannot be volleyed.
2. On the crosscourt return you must get enough angle to get across the court and right into the side at the back of

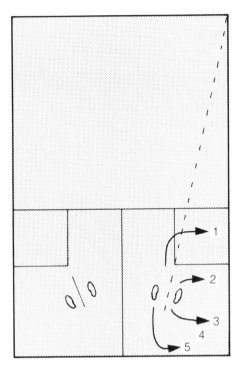

Fig 47   Receiving position: stand a racket length behind the corner of the box, facing the front corner. Look for the receiving options in order of preference.

the service box or even further forward on the side if a volley intercept is threatening.

RECEIVING POSITION

The receiving position (the best place to stand to receive service) is a compromise between being able to volley, to go forward to volley and to take the ball out of the back corners. Your options are:

1. Volley before the ball hits the side.
2. Volley after it hits the side.
3. Drive before the ball hits the back.
4. Drive after it hits the back.
5. Boast.

55

Fig 48 Serving and Receiving. The serve from the left box. The server steps parallel to the short line across the court. Chris Walker, the receiver, stands a racket length back behind the service box with his body facing the front corner but with his head turned to study the serve intently.

To cover these options stand a racket length behind and just outside the back corner of the service box with your toes pointing at the front corner. The imaginary line joining the front corner and box corner will pass between your feet (close to the heel of the right foot).

Stand in the receiving position as you would in the ready position. Turn your head and watch the server.

METHOD

The receiving position is a place you move from. Endeavour to move to the side of the ball and look for your options in the order of preference given.

VARIATIONS

Most of the variations you can use on return of service present themselves on the volley. A loose serve and a quick step forward and you have a range of attacking volleys at your disposal. Generally it is best to play straight and away from the server. Use the straight volley to dying length, the volley kill, the volley drop and vary these with the crosscourt volley nick. Also use the underrated reverse angle volley which will move away from the server.

Very occasionally break the pattern from the back with a drop or reverse angle.

If forced to boast, try a floating boast to give yourself time to cover it.

PRACTICE

If you have a problem on return of serve it is generally because your volley or back corner shots are weak. Improve them with practice. Practise:

1. The straight volley.
2. Throw the ball off the back and boast.

3. Straight drive off the back, solo.
4. Practise boast and crosscourt in pairs.
5. Practise with player A dropping and crosscourting and player B straight volleying and boasting.
6. Practise with player A dropping and straight driving and player B straight driving and boasting.
7. Practise alternating crosscourt, volley, boast.
8. With a partner practise serving and return – ten shots each.
9. Play a three shot rally and stop.

Volley *(Fig 49)*

The volley has moved Jansher Khan from being a great retriever to being a great player. Much of the modern game, aided by modern rackets, is based on the volley, pressure from the volley and volley attack. Get it into your game. Do not let the ball bounce. Look for volleying

Fig 49 The volley: a powerful stance facing the side wall and superb racket head control from Rodney Eyles.

opportunities and like the great master Geoff Hunt, 'hunt the ball'.

PURPOSE
1. Volley to stop the ball going into the back corners. Often players have a problem getting the ball out of the back corners. Volley and stop the ball going in there – eliminate the problem.
2. Volley to dominate the T. Keep the controlling centre position for yourself. Do not move off it if you can help it.
3. Volley to apply pressure. Deprive your opponent of time; the time needed to get to the ball and play good shots. The volleying game is the pressure game.

TARGET AREAS
You are often volleying from the centre of the court. From here you do not need the time a full length gives to recover the T and so you can pull the ball a little shorter. Use a dying length.

However if you are out of position behind your opponent, use a full length.

Get good width on all your crosscourt volleys. Aim for the nick behind the service box on the hard ones.

METHOD
1. Stand half-way between the short line and the front. Position yourself for a straight volley by standing side-on in a basic stance and adjust your feet to get a comfortable distance from the ball. Footwork is important because when reaching vertically it is easy to lose balance or overreach. Do not take too big a step.
2. Racket preparation is crucial as the ball is coming more quickly than off the bounce. Use a short swing preferably at shoulder height.

57

3. The wrist action is 'locked'. Use a short punching action. Push up slightly with an open racket face.
4. Take the ball forward of the body. Push the racket head in a straight line down the line of the shot. Let the elbow move through with the racket head and wrist.
5. Watch the ball right onto the strings.
6. Use an open stance for quick sideways movement on intercepts.

VARIATIONS

The basic volleys can be played at a wide range of places and placements. Two extremes we have are the volley drive, utilizing a full swing, and the volley lob using a short upward push to take the pace off the ball and have it drop in the back corners.

PRACTICE

If volleying does not come easily to you, start right at the beginning with the volley pat exercise (*see* Ball Control).

Next, move to a side-arm action and a side-on position. Hit the ball high and soft, taking plenty of time. Gradually progress back down the court. Start at a level at which you are successful. When you can do twenty at one level you are ready to take another step back. Doing twenty continuously behind the short line without putting your foot over the line is your target. To prove you are an expert try it behind the back of the service box.

ATTACKING SHOTS

Drop Shot *(Figs 50–52)*

The favourite of the connoisseur, the drop is the classic finishing shot to a rally; checkmate in a physical chess battle. The rewards are the points gained and the satisfaction of playing shots. The risks are a string of mistakes. This is your problem. Getting the right balance between the percentage of winners and mistakes.

Do not, as many a 'drop shot artist', overdo it and become readable and predictable. Use the drop when you have two conditions: your opponent is out of position and an easy ball.

OBJECTIVE

1. To move your opponent. The best way to move an opponent is up and down the court.
2. Put your opponent short and look for opportunities to volley while he is out of position.
3. Play winners.

Fig 50   The forehand drop: beautiful preparation from Peter Nicol as he prepares to straight drop against Peter Marshall. Nicol has used his knees to get down to the ball. Note the control of the racket head, the short swing and the open racket face.

Fig 51 The backhand drop: preparation and care from Rodney Martin on the drop as he chooses to attack with his brother Brett out of position behind. Note how he has got down to the ball, the short swing and the open racket face.

TARGET AREAS

1. Play the straight drop to cling, i.e. angled into the side so it stays on and rolls along the wall.
2. Play the crosscourt drop for the nick. This is the crack between the wall and the floor. A dead nick will hit here and roll along the floor.
3. Play the drop low and short. Both 'touch' and 'cut' will bring the drop down into the front corners.
4. Play the ball high enough above the tin so you have a margin for error. Do not aim an inch above the tin. You will make a lot of mistakes. How high do you need to aim to get nine out of ten?

GUIDED METHOD: STRAIGHT DROP

1. Stand with the toe of your front foot on the intersection of the short line and the service box. Point it forward at two o'clock, with your other foot 2ft (60cm) back with toe to the side.
2. Keep your racket low and point it at the back wall, wrist up, racket face open.
3. Drop the ball in front of the line (i.e. slightly in front of your stance) where you can aim it best.
4. Use a short, firm swing with a firm wrist. There is a little bit of a push in the drop. This is down the line of the shot.
5. Use a short follow-through. The speed of the racket head through the ball gives the pace of the shot. At impact you want the racket to be moving slowly and firmly. A follow-through helps this.
6. Play a slow, firm shot to drop onto the front wall. It is a drop shot!

CROSSCOURT

For the crosscourt, crouch low behind the short line on the opposite side of the

Fig 52 The impact position for the forehand straight drop demonstrated.

59

(a)   (b)

Fig 53   The backhand cross-court drop. (a) Hand feed. (b) the open racket to lift the ball and apply cut.

court. Point your front toes to the corner opposite the shot. Keep the ball in front and stroke it across your body to the nick.

VARIATIONS

Vary the drop between straight and crosscourt depending on your opponent's position and which is the most comfortable position for you. We have quickly looked at the basic or touch drops; in the next chapter we will consider cut. We use a blend of both these in our drops, and a range of swings, impact points (e.g. half volley to delayed drop), disguise and deception. There are many drops. Study players with good ones, imitate them and experiment a little.

PRACTICE
1. The touch exercise.
2. The set and cut.
3. The cutting exercise.
4. Feeding and dropping.

Boast *(Figs 54–56)*

The first time I saw Geoff Hunt play I was surprised by how much he boasted. I knew

he drove impeccably and pressurized with the volley but I did not expect the boast.

The boast is the great moving shot; use it to move your opponent around the court. Push your opponent deep, wait for the short ball and boast. Follow up your boast like Hunt and look for the volley.

Fig 54   Sue Wright lets the ball come between herself and the side wall to play one of her famous floating boasts.

Squash is about angles. Do not forget to use them. Get the boast going in your game. Move your opponent.

OBJECTIVE

1. Use the boast to move your opponent diagonally from corner to corner. Try to move your opponent up and down the court rather than side to side.

Fig 55   The forehand boast.

Fig 56   Impact is behind the body so that the ball can be angled into the side wall.

2. 'Follow up on a boast'. Look for the weak ball to volley deep again.

TARGET AREAS

Try to get the second bounce to die in the nick, or on the side. You do not want the ball to sit up comfortably off the side for your opponent or to come out into the middle of the court. Vary the angle on the side to get this right.

GUIDED METHOD

1. Stand as for the drive on the 'sideline' about four inches (10cm) forward of the back of the service box.
2. Turn your toes back slightly and turn on your knees to face the back corner.
3. Throw the ball high off the side to land on the line at the back of the box. Hold your body steady and stroke smoothly across it aiming the ball about 2ft (60cm) behind the intersection of the short line and the side wall.
4. Adjust the horizontal and vertical angles and the height you take the ball, to place it in the corner where it will die.
5. When boasting get used to letting the ball come in between you and the side wall and past you.
6. Use a compact swing and concentrate on control. When in control build up the pace.

VARIATIONS

Many good players use a nick (or three wall) boast from deep in the court. This is hit on a sharper angle and aimed so the

61

first bounce lands in the nick. It is a little risky but can be a winning shot.

FRONT CORNER BOAST

Also called the angle or trickle boast, this just trickles around the front corners.

Move to the side of the ball and prepare as for a straight drive, hold the ball and let it come through. Swing down, hold your racket and wrist back and push the ball into the side wall and follow through normally.

It is not particularly difficult. Set up a few shots and try it off a short swing before you worry about disguising it with delay and a full swing.

PRACTICE

1. Do a little solo practice as outlined above to get used to the angles and placement.
2. Practise boasting and driving with a partner.

Reverse Angle

Point your toes at the front wall in a stance evenly balanced on both feet. Take the ball immediately in front of you and stroke it across your body into the side wall near the front wall to come back across and hit the front wall at a very narrow angle, just above the tin.

This shot stays very close to the front forcing your opponent to move a long way up the court.

Disguise it with the same preparation as a crosscourt from an open stance.

Kill and Hard Low Crosscourt
(Figs 57 & 58)

The kill and the hard, low drive are the ultimate aggressive and finishing shots in squash. Here it is sheer pace that beats an opponent. The speed at which you get to the ball and the speed at which it travels.

Pace is important in squash and so is pressure. Unfortunately players often sacrifice a large degree of control for it. They hit too many too hard, then rush, mistime, make mistakes and play 'loose' shots.

Tactics is about a balance between your hard and soft shots. Pick when you want to hit hard and when you want to hit soft. Pick when you want to go for position and when for pace.

OBJECTIVE

1. To finish a rally by getting the ball to 'die' as quickly as possible.
2. Often it is best played when a player has been pressurized into playing a weak ball that sits up, and is out of position at the back or side of the court.

TARGET AREAS
Straight Kill
1. To die (bounce twice) before the short line.
2. To die on the side wall i.e. angle it in.

Crosscourt Kill
1. To die before the short line and the side.
2. Angle the ball to pass through the front of the service box.

Crosscourt Low Drive
1. To die near the back of the service box. This is faster, wider and dies quicker than a good length or dying length drive. Play it hard across your opponent's body before he has had time to recover or turn.

METHOD
1. For the kill, get into position early so you can take the ball at the top of the bounce.

Fig 57   The high preparation of a kill as Ross Norman prepares to hit down on and through the ball.

Fig 58   Norman takes the ball high and cuts down across the back of it as his racket comes diagonally down. Note the wrist control.

2. Use evenly balanced and upright stance.
3. Take your racket high and swing diagonally down and across your body cutting through the ball.
4. Taking the ball high allows you to hit down on it so that it will land shorter on the court. Cut will also help to pull it down.

This shot will not give you recovery time so generally play it only when you are well positioned to recover.

VARIATIONS
An alternative to the kill is the 'nick' kill. Here the ball is played as a kill and driven straight into the nick and rolls out along the floor. The result can be spectacular but the risks of 'tinning' the ball or having it 'sit' up and leave you out of position are considerable. Do not get carried away attempting it, and know when to stop playing it if it is not working.

If an opportunity presents itself to kill where you have time, an element of deception to 'wrong foot' an opponent can be useful as a large part of the success of the shot is beating a turning player.

PRACTICE
Opportunities for the kill present themselves rarely. A little pairs practice with a coach or partner feeding from behind (high and very soft) can allow you to get used to the diagonal path of the swing and groove the shot.

BACK CORNERS

Squash is a game of strict levels and nowhere are they outlined more clearly than the back corners.

The first problem for the beginner is getting the ball into the back corner. The second is getting it out. Their game will hit a plateau until they do this satisfactorily. The next stage is not just getting it out but being able to play a safe, tight straight drive to good length. We could further this to the ability to drive hard and play various attacking shots and variations from this position, but the key is how well and 'tight' you can recover from the back corners.

The first shot you learn is a boast. As soon as you progress to being able to straight drive your game goes up a level.

How good you become as a player depends largely on how well you get the ball into and out of the back corners.

Objective

1. The first opportunity you look for in the back corners is the straight drive. It is dangerous to boast especially if your opponent has the T. The ball can be relatively easy to get to, and can be dropped to force you to run the whole diagonal. Play the straight if you can. Win the T and put your opponent out of position in the back.
2. If you cannot straight drive you are forced to boast, a situation to avoid if possible. If you are in position you should be able to get the ball straight by taking it either before the back or after it has rebounded off the back wall.

Method

BOAST *(Figs 59–61)*
1. Stand one and a half racket lengths from the back wall on an imaginary line joining the back of the half-court line with the corner of the service box.
2. Face the corner. The 'line' between your feet will be directly at the corner. Use a 'back corner' stance.
3. Throw the ball high and soft to come off the back and land on the line between you and the corner. (If it is a poor throw, stop and throw again.)
4. Prepare your racket before you throw. Use a compact swing with an open racket face, come under the ball and lift it into the side wall just inside the service box.
5. Bend your knees to help get under the ball and maintain balance.
6. To place the ball where you wish, vary the angle you aim on the side, the height and the pace.

STRAIGHT DRIVE *(Figs 62 & 63)*
1. Position for the boast.
2. Throw the ball high to come out level with the front foot.
3. Turn a little on the knees and hold your body steady facing the side.
4. Swing across your body and lift the ball high up on the wall to land in the area behind the service box.

(a)   (b)   (c)

Fig 59   The back corner boast: forehand. (a) Preparation. (b) Impact. (c) Follow-through.

(a)	(b)	(c)

Fig 60 (above) The back corner boast: backhand. (a) Positioning, preparation and hand feeding. (b) Getting down under the ball. Note the open racket face. (c) Impact. Good balance and distance from the ball.

Fig 61   (right) Boast: position yourself so that the ball is between you and your corner.

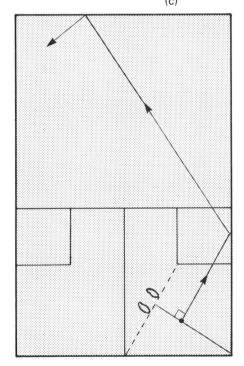

5. If the ball does not come out enough you must move to the side of it and endeavour to get round behind it.
6. Skill. Throw ten balls off the back. How many shots can you get to land back behind the service box?

GENERAL

The key to getting the ball out of the back is positioning. From the T position turn around and face the corner. Move to the side of the ball, not at it. Swing under the ball and lift it.

Two advanced techniques that can allow you to get the most difficult balls straight are firstly to use more 'wrist' to accelerate and lift the ball, and secondly to use a shorter grip.

PRACTICE

1. Solo – single shot skills test.
2. Solo – continuously.
3. Pairs – circling.

VARIATIONS

Caution should be urged in attempting variations from the backcourt. This is a defensive situation. Safety and patience are the prime requirements. It is easy to see from the balcony where over-ambi-

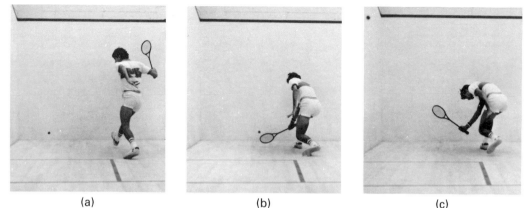

(a)   (b)   (c)

Fig 62   The back corner forehand straight drive demonstrated by Jansher Khan. (a) As Jansher moves to the back for the low ball he prepares his racket and starts to get down to the ball. (b) Reaching back for the ball with his weight on the back foot Jansher gets low and pulls the elbow down for a lower backswing. Note how he has moved parallel to the ball. (c) Coming under and up on the ball Jansher swivels and manages to get it straight.

tious shots lead to mistakes or put the player in a poor position.

Variations, however, can be used to vary play (e.g. vary length, pace, crosscourt and lob), to surprise (drops, reverse angles, boasts) or to break up a pattern (kills or skid boasts).

It is often best to play several long shots until your opponent is lagging back slightly before surprising with a short shot. Attack from the back when your opponent is:

1. Back off the T.
2. Watching the front wall.
3. Turning so his toes face the side.
4. Back on his heels.
5. Very tired.

When rallying down the walls, vary length shots, occasionally play a shorter

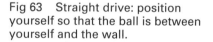

Fig 63   Straight drive: position yourself so that the ball is between yourself and the wall.

ball that restricts an opponent moving from the T, to a straight drive or boast. Pick crosscourt shots carefully so as not to provide opponents with easy volleying opportunities.

3
Advanced Shots and Techniques

ADDED DIMENSIONS

My favourite question for the novice coach is: what is the difference between disguise and deception? You can use these two in your game plus something few other games offer – angles. Add to these the dimensions of placement (length, width and height) and the variations of pace and spin available and you have a whole range of shots and problems with which to present your opponent.

You may not be able to emulate the magic of Brett Martin, but be prepared to learn and develop new shots. Observe, experiment and practice. There is only one rule: if it works consistently use it.

Squash is a percentage game. It is not the isolated miracle that is going to make you a better player. Work on a shot, practise it systematically and work it into your game at the right time. Here are some ideas you can try.

Spin

CUT

Cut or backspin has two advantages. Firstly, it allows you to play the ball quickly while taking the pace off it. Secondly, imparting cut will allow you to play a little higher over the tin and pull the ball down more to the floor where it will die shorter.

Fig 64   Chris Walker about to cut down on the ball goes on the attack against Rodney Martin.

Cut is used primarily on the cut drops and volley drops. Use it also on the kills and low drives.

To cut the ball, use a short or compact swing. Hold the racket face open with a firm wrist and push down as well as through. Listen for the cutting sound.

Practise cutting by setting the ball high and soft close to the front and cutting down on it just above the tin. Repeat this, it is the 'set and cut' exercise. Next progress to cutting continuously. This is the 'cutting' exercise. When practising 'feel' your racket head at the end of the shot and see if you still have control of it.

The Pakistanis brought cut into the game. Rodney Martin mastered it and led the modern attacking style of the game. Cut has become a prime requisite in the modern attacking game. Davenport uses it brilliantly on his volley intercepts. Practise and get it into your game.

TOPSPIN

This is little used in squash but is still useful on the opportunist half volley and the deceptive rolled drop.

It allows you to take the ball on the rise safely by closing the racket face and smothering the ball.

Touch

Touch is the special ability of being able to hit the ball very softly.

To achieve touch the racket must be travelling slowly at impact. It is difficult to time a large slow swing to connect with the ball. A short swing moving early in slow motion will provide touch.

Another possibility is to pull your swing. You achieve this by swinging at normal speed and 'braking' the stroke through the impact point.

Practise by using the 'touch' practice. Stand close to the front and practise lifting the ball just above the tin. Use an open face and a side-arm stroke with the wrist up rather than an under-arm one, and come under the ball.

Touch can be used on the drops, volley drops, lobs, service and floating boasts.

The Egyptians are the masters of touch. Squash is a game of hard and soft shots. Don't forget the soft ones. Get touch into your game.

Disguise

With disguise you endeavour to 'shape' (prepare) in the same way for each shot. This disguises it to the extent that your opponent won't know where it is going until the ball is actually played.

For example, the positioning and racket preparation can be the same for the forehand straight drive, crosscourt and front corner boast. Practise this by getting into one position from which you can play each shot.

When you have time you can move to the disguised position early and from there move to the best position for the shot. For example, move to the disguised position in the forehand front corner, hold it and then move to a short swing from the drop.

Don't overrate disguise, or let it spoil your shots. It is a good thing to have in your game but you don't need it all the time. Use it more when your opponent is in position on the T.

Surprise

Disguise is most effective when it is used in conjunction with surprise. Of the total range of shots you have available in a certain position (the variations) you will use some more than others. Your play will follow a pattern. Set up this pattern, then suddenly alter it by using another perhaps including disguise, deception or a change of pace.

1. If a crosscourt has been the standard reply to a boast, then a quick straight drive would provide surprise.

2. A quick reverse angle volley could surprise a server expecting a straight volley.

3. Shaping for a straight drive to follow your pattern from the back corner could wrong foot your opponent.

The variations are unlimited. Build up your repertoire but don't overdo it.

Deception *(Fig 66)*

With deception you show your opponent the shot you are shaping to play, delay, and then change it to another shot. Hopefully, your opponent will have already moved for the first shot (or at least transferred his weight) making it difficult or too late to turn or change direction.

Delay is necessary for deception. You can be absolutely brilliant in providing a mirage of flamboyant strokes, but if your opponent hasn't moved you are missing the point.

Fig 65   Australian Brett Martin is a master at shaping for one shot and using his wrist to play another. Here he wrong foots Chris Walker with a straight drop played from out in front of the body.

The wrist is the key to deception. The position of the body, the backswing and the swing 'show' the stroke, and the wrist changes it at the last minute.

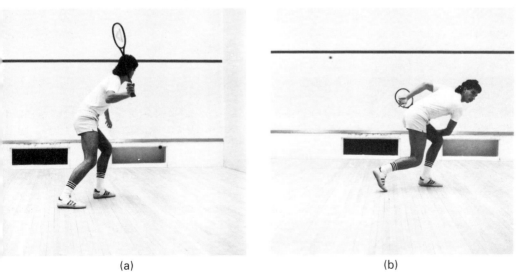

(a)   (b)

Fig 66   (a) The striker shapes for a straight drive and holds it.
(b) Turning his body to the side and with a clever turn of the head, he uses his wrist to flick the ball crosscourt. A perfect deception.

69

Body deception through turning the body and head with the 'show' stroke also helps to deceive the opponent.

For the crosscourt drop, shape and hold for the straight drop, keep the ball a little forward and just before impact break the wrist slightly and flick the ball across court. You will sacrifice a little control and feel but the results can be well worth while.

MAIN AREAS OF DECEPTION

1. Shaping to hit straight and hitting across. Use wrist and body deception.
2. Shaping to hit across and hitting straight. Use wrist and body deception.
3. Shaping to hit long and hitting short. Use full swing to short swing.
4. Shaping to hit short and hitting long. Use short swing to flick.

There are many other variations. Study the players who use them. Try them out in practice. I know a good deceptive shot looks spontaneous, but I practise them with my pupils and we get them right before venturing into matches with them.

In a close game where the points are hard to come by, deception could just provide the finishing touch. The great players use it. Jansher Khan has learnt it. Rodney Martin regularly makes his opponents move forward while he hits back. Brett Martin mesmerizes them with brilliant wrist deception and clever changes of body position. Zaman was brilliantly attacking and deceptive. Jahangir's game was a frightening blend of power and deception. Practise and you can have it too.

Variations

Squash is a game of shots and angles. This is your armoury. The more weapons at your disposal, the more successful you are likely to be.

The more variations you can winkle out of a situation the more chance you have of beating your opponent. Use variations with disguise.

Fig 67 shows some of the variations from the front court.

1. Straight drop.
2. Crosscourt drop (also the deceptive 'faded' crosscourt drop).
3. Front corner boast.
4. Reverse angle.
5. Crosscourt kill (also kill to crosscourt nick and crosscourt low drive).
6. Straight kill (also straight low drive).
7. Straight drive for length (also for dying length).
8. Crosscourt drive for length (also for dying length).

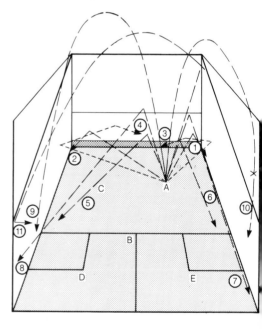

Fig 67   Variations from the front court.

9. Crosscourt lob.
10. Straight lob.
11. Corkscrew lob.

Of the available variations work out the best alternatives in order of preference if your opponent is in position B, C, D or E.

Fig 68 shows some of the variations from the back court.

1. Straight drive.
2. Crosscourt drive.
3. Crosscourt lob.
4. Boast (and nick boast).
5. Straight drop.
6. Crosscourt drop (and also the deceptive crosscourt drop).
7. Straight kill.
8. Crosscourt kill.
9. Reverse angle.
10. Skid boast.

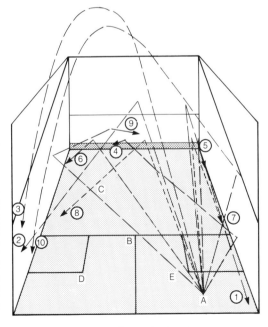

Fig 68   Variations from the back court.

Of all the available variations work out the best alternatives in order of preference if your opponent is in position B, C, D or E.

RECOVERY SHOTS

Squash is about getting the ball back and getting it back safely. When you are under pressure it is easy to attempt a non-percentage shot (i.e. go for a lucky winner) and it is often hard to play a defensive shot that will give you time to recover the T. Here are some of the shots you can use.

Flick Lob

When you are stretched to the front, as soon as your foot goes down you want to be ready to lob. If you are stretched too far and you haven't time for a backswing, take your racket low, under the ball and open your racket face. Use your wrist to flick and lift the ball high to drop in the back corner. The flick lob is seen regularly in the athletic retrieving of Ross Norman. He seems to need only inches of backswing but gets the ball away high and safely.

Back Wall Boast

If you push right up on the T to look for the intercept, occasionally a ball may pass you that will die before the back wall and will not give you time to get behind for a straight drive or boast.

This is where you use the back wall boast or what could be more usefully called, a back wall lob. Practise it by throwing the ball off the back and swinging it firmly down under the ball, lifting it as high on the back as possible. With luck and a little practice the ball will hit the front near the side and fade in to cling.

Cling Lob

When really under pressure you may feel you do not have the control to risk playing the lob into the side wall as it may go out. An alternative that is a little 'looser' but much safer is to bring the lob high to the back wall first and then have it bounce and move into the side. Ideally it will move in to cling.

High Drop

When Jansher Khan is so stretched in the front court that he cannot lob, he does not push in a low drop that would not give any recovery time, but uses a high drop, several feet high, even up by the cut line. Really, this is a little lob that stays in the front court and gives him some time to get back behind an opponent and into a ready position to look for the intercept.

Jansher is devastatingly fast so it works for him, but if you have no other alternative you could try it. The secret is to play the shot so tight that it clings.

Extra Width *(Fig 69)*

Occasionally, because of your position in relation to the ball you are committed to play a crosscourt but your opponent is in position and looking for the intercept. In this situation you must hit the side wall before he can volley. This shot will bounce out behind him into the court and although he may recover it, you should be back in position. Play wide crosscourts when your opponent is on the T.

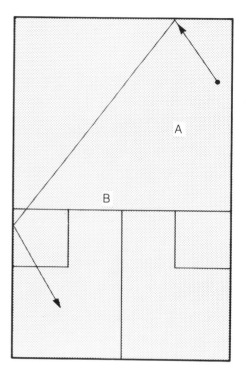

Fig 69   A is stretched and can't play straight. B has moved up to look for the volley. A counters with extra width.

ANGLES

Skid Boast *(Fig 70)*

If your opponent is in control on the T and hanging into your side of the court with the ball behind you so you cannot crosscourt, you can consider the skid boast.

Hit the ball more like a high hard straight drive than a boast. Touch the side wall so the ball comes high on the front and across to hit the opposite side behind the opposite service box.

Brett Martin uses this shot to turn defence into attack.

This shot is easily practised by two players feeding straight and skid boasting.

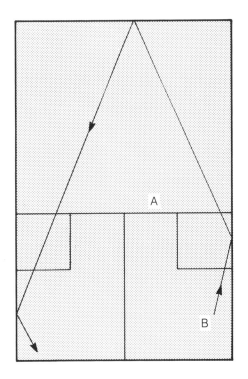

Fig 70   The skid boast.

Floating Boast

When forced to boast, you can use touch and lift the ball in a lobbing fashion so it drops down onto the front wall and stays close to the front. This shot takes time and like the lob gives you time to recover the T. It drags an opponent right out of position into the front corners.

THE ATTACKING VOLLEYS

Much of squash can be seen as a continual pursuit of the opportunities to finish rallies. Many of these opportunities will occur when an opponent is caught out of position by a ball taken early.

There are two actions used in the attacking volley – the side-on action (*see* Chapter 2) and the overhead smash action, which is like a tennis serve or overarm throw.

On attacking volleys we are hitting down through the ball in order to play it short, so

(a)   (b)   (c)

Fig 71   The smash: (a) Jansher prepares for a smash action like a tennis serve by taking the racket high and behind his head. (b) At impact the racket comes up behind and over the ball to hit down to the opposite front nick, (c) and the racket travels down across the body.

Fig 72 Jahangir Khan reaches high and attacks with a straight backhand volley.

generally the path of the swing will have the racket start above the ball and move diagonally down through it. A chopping action to impart cut, braked through impact, is often used but in many cases the ball will almost bounce off the racket to the front and die.

Volley Drop

Start with a high backswing and, using a short swing, chop at the ball. On the straight volley drop, use a margin for error above the tin, up to 6in (15cm), and play the ball to bounce and cling. If the ball is well out from the side you may be able to get an appropriate angle to hit the nick.

A good opportunity to volley drop is off a crosscourt from behind as it can be played tightly off high, loose drives.

Stop Volley

This is a very simple volley drop played with a still racket or a little push. Often a player hardly needs to swing at the ball but just get the racket to it.

| (a) | (b) | (c) |

Fig 73 The straight backhand volley drop: (a) preparation, (b) impact with cut and touch. Note the firm wrist. (c) Follow-through, still with the firm wrist and a target area just above the tin that allows a margin 'for error' and room so that the ball can be angled in to the nick or to cling.

Volley Kill

The volley kill is hit hard, preferably with cut, to die short. Swing diagonally down through the ball. Position around to the side on straight volley kills so that you will not pull the ball out from the side.

Volley Crosscourt Nicks

The volley crosscourt nick, often played overhead, is a spectacular, if somewhat risky shot. On the forehand use a smash action when the ball is high and swing diagonally down and across the body.

This shot can be used on both sides, and is often attempted on the return of serve but it is an easy way to waste points and must be stopped if it is not working.

Volley Boast

This is a highly effective yet underrated shot ideally used on loose straight drives when an opponent is behind. Position as for the boast but use a short swing to turn the ball into the side. It is easily practised

Fig 74   Volley boast and drive.

in the pairs exercise, boast and drive.

Volley Reverse Angle

There is a neat little opportunity to use the volley reverse angle on a loose serve. Really the receiver needs to face the front, get into line with the ball and hit across his body so that the ball hits low on the opposite side wall and rebounds across the court just above the tin. Take care!

Practising

Attacking volleys are easily practised solo by feeding the ball up and playing the shot. To practise straight attacking volleys stand outside the service box by the short line and feed high and soft so the ball comes between you and the wall; pick an appropriate ball and volley drop.

Crosscourt volley nicks are easily practised by feeding straight off the front wall so the ball sits up overhead or alternatively using the corner volley exercise, to keep the ball warm for feeding.

The volley drop off the crosscourt can be practised where player A behind feeds a crosscourt for B to volley drop and drive. Player B then feeds from the other side.

Corkscrew Lob

The ultimate use of angles in squash is with the corkscrew lob.

When the ball sits up in the front of the court, get under it and hit as hard, high and close to the side as possible on the front wall. With practice and a hot ball you can get it crosscourt to hit the side wall close to the back and come out parallel inches off the back and nearly impossible to get. Take a big step into the middle and try it on the service.

4
Skills Tests

HOW TO USE THE TESTS

These tests are designed to provide you with a progressive system of targets so you can assess your skill level and the results of your practice.

You will be able to identify weaknesses and work on these. It will also help you to concentrate on accuracy and consistency in your practice.

Scoring

Score each exercise strictly, stopping when you hit the ball outside the target area, step over a line or use the wrong shot (e.g. backhand instead of forehand).

Progress to the next skill level when you can pass each exercise and total over seventy-five per cent.

In the Test

Use the appropriate speed ball. One short practice is allowed before the continuous exercises and three trial shots before the single shot exercises. The continuous exercises are best of three attempts. (FH is forehand, BH is backhand.)

Your Percentage Skill

For each level work this out by dividing your total score by two.

SKILLS TEST 1: BEGINNER *(Fig 75)*
1. *Drives* Continuously drive above cut line until error occurs. Score up to thirty.
2. *Volleys* Continuously any distance from wall. Score up to twenty.
3. *Single corner exercise* Right corner. BH front/side, FH side/front continuously. Left corner. FH front/side, BH side/front continuously.

Exercise		Max Score	Pass Rate	Personal Scores	
1	FH	30	15		
	BH	30	15		
2	FH	20	10		
	BH	20	10		
3	R	20	10		
	L	20	10		
4	R	10	5		
	L	10	5		
5	FH	10	5		
	BH	10	5		
6	FH	10	5		
	BH	10	5		
TOTAL		200	150		
% SKILL (= total ÷ 2)		100	75		

Fig 75

76

4. *Service* Score good serves that hit side wall and land behind short line. Out of ten attempts.
5. *Drop straight* From behind the short line bounce the ball and play a drop to land within one racket length of the side wall and four lengths of the front wall. Score out of ten.
6. *Back corner boast* Throw ball off back wall. Boast must hit front wall below cut line and opposite side wall before or after bounce. Score out of ten.

SKILLS TEST 2: INTERMEDIATE *(Fig 76)*

1. *Drives* Continuous drives behind the short line until error occurs. Score up to thirty.
2. *Volleys* Continuously behind a chalk line four racket lengths from the front wall. Score up to twenty.
3. *The corner exercise* From the T play a forehand crosscourt to hit front wall, then side to rebound into middle. Backhand crosscourt to opposite front corner. Alternate forehand and backhand continuously to thirty.
4. *Service* Score good serves that hit the side wall and land in area behind and within width of service box. Score out of ten attempts.
5. *Drops: crosscourt* From behind the short line and on the opposite side of the half-court line, set the ball up off the front and drop to land within one racket length of the side wall and four lengths from the front wall.
6. *Back corners* Throw the ball off the back wall and hit high on front wall to land in area behind and within width of service box. Score out of fifteen.

	Exercise	Max Score	Pass Rate	Personal Scores	
1	FH	30	10		
	BH	30	10		
2	FH	20	10		
	BH	20	10		
3		30	10		
4	R	10	5		
	L	10	5		
5	FH	10	5		
	BH	10	5		
6	FH	15	7		
	BH	15	7		
TOTAL		200	150		
% SKILL (= total ÷ 2)		100	75		

Fig 76

SKILLS TEST 3: ADVANCED *(Fig 77)*

1. *Drives* Throw ball off back and drive continuously to land behind and within width of the service box, i.e. ball may be struck before or after back wall. Rebounds off back wall allowed. Continuously to thirty.
2. *Volley* Staying completely behind short line play continuous volleys to twenty.
3. *Corner volleys* Forehand crosscourt to hit front wall, then side to rebound into middle to be volleyed backhand across to opposite front wall then side. Continuous to thirty.
4. *Double corner exercise* From the T play a forehand crosscourt to hit front wall, then side to rebound into middle. Backhand to same corner front then side. Backhand to opposite front corner. Forehand to same corner. Repeat. Continuous to thirty.

Exercise		Max Score	Pass Rate	Personal Scores	
1	FH	30	10		
	BH	30	10		
2	FH	20	10		
	BH	20	10		
3		30	10		
4		30	10		
5	R	10	3		
	L	10	3		
6	FH	5	2		
	BH	5	2		
	FH	5	2		
	BH	5	2		
TOTAL		200	150		
% SKILL (= total ÷ 2)		100	75		

Fig 77

Exercise		Max Score	Pass Rate	Personal Scores	
1	FH	20	10		
	BH	20	10		
(a) 2	FH	20	10		
	BH	20	10		
(b)		20	10		
3		20	10		
4	FH	20	10		
	BH	20	10		
5	FH	10	4		
	BH	10	4		
6	FH	10	4		
	BH	10	4		
TOTAL		200	150		
% SKILL (= total ÷ 2)		100	75		

Fig 78

5. *Service* Score attempts out of ten that hit side, floor then back.
6. *Drops* Set ball up front/side to rebound into the middle. From behind the short line play drops straight and crosscourt to land within one racket length of the side wall and three racket lengths of the front.

SKILLS TEST 4: ELITE *(Fig 78)*
1. *Drives* Continuously to land in the service box alternating one above the cut line and one below.
2. *Volleys* (a) Continuously behind service box. (b) Continuously behind short line with forehand and backhand returning directly from the front.

3. *Boasting* Continuously boasting in the front corners with the ball bouncing before the side wall and then rebounding off, before being boasted again.
4. *Screw drives* Continuously straight drive for the ball to hit the front/side and screw out into the middle.
5. *Volley drops* Staying behind the short line feed the ball off the front wall and volley drop straight to land within one racket width and three lengths of the front wall.
6. *Drops* Drive the ball to bounce and then rebound off the back wall and then drop to land within one racket width and three lengths of the front wall.

5
Solo Practice

Playing squash is a good way to maintain your standard. It is not the best way to develop your technique, shots and skills.

Squash players are lucky that they can get on court and practise by themselves. It is a wonderful game for the sports person who is motivated, organized, interested and disciplined enough to practise and improve.

Solo practice can improve your ball control and technique. It can also improve your shots and the accuracy and consistency of these shots – your skills. Firstly concentrate on technique, secondly on placement and thirdly, where appropriate, pace.

Practice Session

1. *Appointment* Make a specific time to practise and discipline yourself to keep to it. Use other opportunities as they occur. Two players can solo practise using half the court each.
2. *Set goals* The more specific your practice goals are the better. Write them down. Use the skill tests. Work out exactly what you are trying to achieve. Do not just practise what you are good at and your favourite things. Work on your weaknesses too.
3. *Plan it* Build up the time so you can concentrate for forty minutes.

   Use one of the practice sequences or plan your own. Write it down. Plan the length of time you spend on each shot. Concentrate on a few main areas. Use repetition. *See* the section on learning a skill in Chapter 7.
4. *Balance it* Use a balance of continuous, single shot, moving and static exercises. Have some variety, and then come back to the main theme. Remember you can work on technique, shots skills and movement.
5. *Be flexible* Before a tournament you may want to be comprehensive about your practice and stick to your planned routine, but if you are practising to develop shots and skills and something is working particularly well then you can concentrate on it. Learning goes in spurts and plateaus. If you are in a spurt, stick with it.
6. *Be systematic* Repetition is the key to skill learning. Repeat the same feed and shot again and again and then come back to it. Do not use a hotchpotch of shots and feeds. Remember you are grooving your shots.

Practising

FEEDING
There are a large number of feeding situations in which you can self feed the ball to practise various shots.

Use the feeding progression (i.e. hand feeding the ball, bouncing it, throwing it off the side, setting it up with a single shot off the front or front/side and the whole range of continuous practices).

Ideally you want the ball to come back to you after the shot you have practised to keep the exercise moving.

CONTINUOUS EXERCISES
I use a number of front court and continuous driving exercises for technique, control, movement and to feed balls.

SKILLS TESTS
Use the skills tests to help assess your level, and provide targets.

PRACTICES

(*See also* Technique Practices)

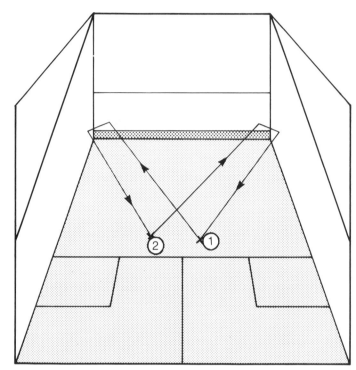

Fig 79   The corner exercise or corner screws: (1) forehand crosscourt front/side; (2) backhand crosscourt front/side.

Front Court Practices

1. *The corner exercise* Corner crosscourt front/side to screw out for a backhand to the opposite front corner.
   (a) Above the cut line.
   (b) Below the cut line.
2. *Screw drives* Straight front/side to screw out into the middle. Forehand and backhand.
3. *Double corner exercise* Forehand crosscourt front/side, backhand straight front/side, backhand crosscourt front/side, forehand straight front/side, and so on.
   (a) Above the cut line.
   (b) Below the cut line.

4. *Reverse angles*
   (a) Crosscourt side/front to bounce, hit opposite side and repeat. Forehand and backhand.
   (b) Crosscourt side/front to bounce and repeat (i.e. hit before side). Forehand and backhand.
5. *Boasting* Continuous boasting side to side, one forehand and one backhand.
   (a) To rebound directly off the side wall and repeat.
   (b) To bounce on the floor before rebounding. In this exercise use a very hot or fast ball. Initially the ball may have to bounce twice occasionally.

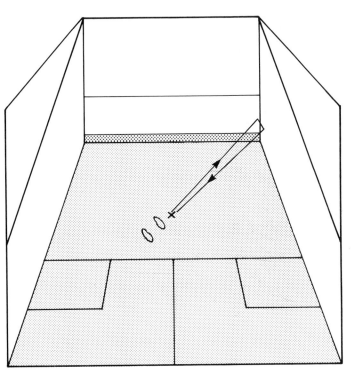

Fig 80   Screw drives: forehand front/side continuously.

9. *Set and cut* Set the ball up quite high close to the front wall and cut from the top of the bounce. Repeat. Forehand and backhand.

10. *Cutting exercise* Continuously cut the ball just above the tin. Use your feet, a fast backswing and a firm wrist. Forehand and backhand.

There are four basic drops: forehand straight and crosscourt and backhand straight and crosscourt. You can use touch or cut or a combination of both. (*See* Basic Shots and the Skills Tests.)
    (a) Hand feed and drop.
    (b) Set the ball up off the front and drop.
    (c) Set the ball up front/side and drop.

6. *Reflex drives* Fast low drives in front of short line. Use fast racket preparation, a firm wrist, fast footwork and compact swing. Forehand and backhand.

7. *Single corner exercise*
    (a) Right Corner. Forehand side/front, backhand front/side.
    (b) Left Corner. Backhand side/front. Forehand front/side.

8. *Touch exercise* Very close to the front use a short swing with an open racket face below the ball. With a firm slow swing lift the ball a few feet above the tin. Play the ball as softly as possible, gradually getting lower, bend your knees, move your feet and use a very rapid backswing. Forehand and backhand.

11. *Drops* Drive two or three times to the short line and then drop – repeat.

12. *Drops and corners* Feed backhand crosscourt front/side and drop.
    (a) Forehand straight, then forehand crosscourt front/side and repeat.
    (b) Forehand crosscourt and repeat. Feed a forehand crosscourt front/side and drop.
    (c) Backhand straight, then backhand crosscourt front/side and repeat.
    (d) Backhand crosscourt and repeat.

The corner exercise can be used several times between each shot or between groups of shots.

81

13. *Boasts*
    (a) Hand feeds at back of service box and boast. (*See* the section on shots in Chapter 2.) Forehand and backhand.
    (b) Drive to service box three times and boast so second bounce dies in nick. Set ball to opposite box after a few bounces and repeat.
14. *Back corner boast*
    (a) Throw ball off back wall and boast, forehand and backhand.
    (b) Drive to back and boast. Forehand and backhand.
15. *Kills*
    (a) Feed to short line; kill straight. Forehand and backhand.
    (b) Set with corner shots and kill to nick. Forehand and backhand, straight and crosscourt.
    (c) Drive for length and kill off back. (Straight and crosscourt.)

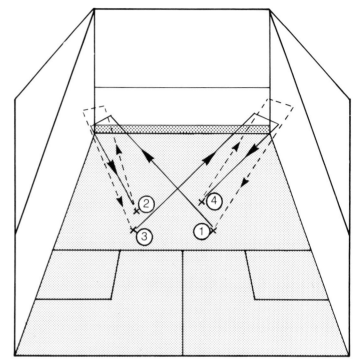

Fig 81   Double screws: (1) forehand crosscourt front/side; (2) backhand straight front/side; (3) backhand crosscourt front/side; (4) forehand straight front/side.

Volley Practices

1. *Short volleys* Half-way between short line and front wall, volley continuously.
2. *Volleys* Behind short line, volley continuously.
3. *Moving volleys*
    (a) Moving up and down the court front to back.
    (b) Moving side to side. Play straight volleys then feed crosscourt, run, and volley straight and repeat.
4. *Volley corner exercise*
    (a) Above the cut line (forehand crosscourt front/side to rebound out and then backhand out to opposite corner).
    (b) Below cut line.
5. *Double volley exercise* As for double corner exercise.
6. *Alternating volleys*
    (a) Half-way from the short line to the front alternate forehand and backhand volleys.
    (b) Behind the short line (ball coming directly from front).
7. *Reflex volleys* Half-way to the front, volley continuously as hard and fast as possible.

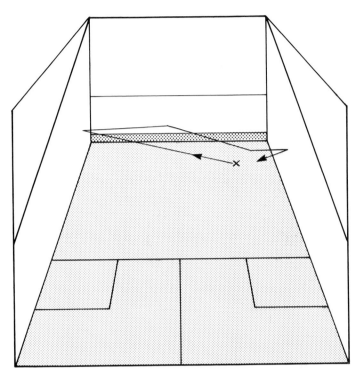

Fig 82   Reverse angle: forehand crosscourt side/front.

Drive Practices

1. *Length* Take the ball off the back and lift above the cut line. Get into a smooth rhythm.
2. *Length and dying length* Take one ball off the back and one before the back.
3. *High drives* Aim the ball just under the out of court line.
4. *Hard and soft* Play one drive hard and the next soft.
5. *Hard drives* Play all drives as hard as possible while keeping control.
6. *Crosscourt drives* Drive straight and pick the ball that comes off the back a little more to crosscourt. Play to hit side, floor, back and repeat on the other side.

Play the crosscourts:
(a) High and soft.
(b) Wide and medium pace.
(c) Hard.

8. *Reflex alternating volleys* As for alternating volleys but very fast. Half-way between the short line and the front.
9. *Volley drops*
   (a) Feed from hand (from short line).
   (b) Single feed and volley drop.
   (c) Volley continuously and volley drop.
10. *Volley drops* From 'corners'.
11. *Volley nicks* Set high and use a smash action. Forehand and backhand straight and crosscourt.
12. *Volley boasts*
   (a) Feed from hand, second bounce in nick.
   (b) Volley straight several times and volley boast. Repeat on opposite side.

Sequences

BEGINNERS LEVEL I
See Technique Sequence I

SHOT PRACTICE SEQUENCE I
Short drives FH. Above cut line × 2 min.
Service Right box × 10
Short drives BH. Above cut line × 2 min.
Service Left box × 10
Single corner ex. Right corner × 2 min.
Drops Hand feed FH straight from short line × 10

Single corner ex. Left corner × 12min.
Drops BH straight × 10
Service box drives FH × 3 min.
Boasts FH feed at back of service box × 10
Service box drives BH × 3 min.
Boasts BH hand feed at back of service box × 10
Volleys FH × 2 min.
Back corner boast × 10
Service box drives FH × 3 min.
Service box drives BH × 3 min.
Total approx. 40 min.

This is a very full sequence and it may be better to use half of it first until you are familiar with the exercises.

INTERMEDIATE LEVEL II
See Technique Sequence II.

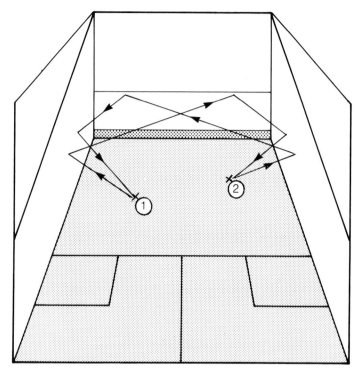

Fig 83   Boasting: (1) backhand boast; (2) forehand boast.

SHOT PRACTICE SEQUENCE II
Service box drives FH × 3 min.
Service Right box × 10
Service box drives BH × 3 min.
Service Left box × 10
Corner ex. × 2 min.
Drops Set off front wall and play a FH straight drop × 10
Corner ex. × 2 min.
Drops Set off front. BH straight drop × 10
Boasts Drive continually to service box and boast and repeat on opposite side × 20
Volley FH half-way from short line to front × 2 min.
Back corners Throw ball off back wall and drive straight for length. FH × 10
Volley BH × 2 min.

Back corners BH × 10
Corners ex. × 3 min.
Total approx 35 min.

ADVANCED & ELITE LEVEL III & IV
See Technique Sequence III

FRONT COURT SEQUENCE
Corners
Boasting Front corner to rebound off side.
Single corner ex. Right corner
Double corners
Single corner ex. Right corner
Double
Single corner ex. Left corner
Touch ex. FH

Double corner exercise
Touch ex. BH
Corners
Drops FH Straight, screw feed.
Corners
Drops BH Straight, screw feed.
Double corner exercise
Drops FH crosscourt.
Double corner exercise
Drops BH crosscourt.
Boasts Front corner to bounce on floor before rebounding.

There are an unlimited number of sequences you can build on using the continuous exercises, feeding progression and shots. Try to build your own with a theme, concentrating on drops, touch, cut, speed, kills, volleys, boasts and so on.

VOLLEY SEQUENCE
(Basic volleys and volley drops; two to three minutes each exercise.)

Short volleys FH and BH.
Volleys FH and BH.
Moving volleys Side to side.
Volley corners
Alternating volleys From front and short line.
Volley drops Feed off front and drop FH, BH.
Reflex volleys
Double volley exercise
Reflex alternating volleys

DRIVE SEQUENCE
(Length and crosscourts; two to three times each exercise.)

Length drives FH and BH.
Straight and crosscourt drives High.
Length and dying length FH and BH.
Straight and crosscourt drives Medium.
Hard and soft FH and BH.
Straight and crosscourt drives Hard.

The straight drives could be fed to the service box and crosscourted or taken off the back wall and then crosscourted.

YOUR SEQUENCES
Use the exercises and shots above to develop your own sequences. Write them down and take them on court with you.

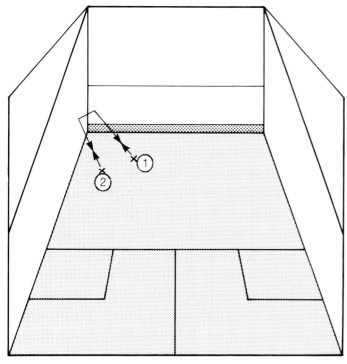

Fig 84   Single corner exercise: (1) forehand front/side; (2) backhand side/front.

6

Pairs Practice and Practice Games

Regular pairs practice is vital for any serious player. The best way to improve is not to play match after match but to improve the things you are doing in your matches.

Pairs practice is the next step, after solo practice. It allows you to practise technique, a greater range of shots, movement and to work under pressure.

Work out exactly what you want in terms of technique, movement and the target area. Concentrate on one aspect at a time. Keep working on it until it is working well and then move on. Start slowly and try to get into a rhythm in your practice. Gradually build up the pressure. When the shots are working well in practice, try them in a condition game.

Condition games provide practice at specific shots and combinations in a game situation. An unkind friend of mine calls them 'con' games because I always make the rules!

Practice games allow you to work things into your game without the pressure of a match. This is where you can work on your game and develop it.

PAIRS PRACTICES

1. *Knock-up*
   (a) Technique practice. Try as a target area the intersection of the service box line with the short line. This is not a shot, it is an exercise. Step back from each ball every time, move your feet, get in the best position, prepare for your shot and groove your swing. Practise your best hitting.
   (b) Length and crosscourt. Hit several lengths down the side and pick the ball to crosscourt, to hit the side, floor, then back, for your partner to repeat on the opposite side. *Scoring.* Score a point each time you hit the target area (side, floor, back). Who can get the most points? Alternatively, feed to the service box and then crosscourt.

2. *Boast and drive*
   (a) Attacking boast. A straight drives to the service box and B boasts, A repeats the drive on the opposite side, B boasts and so on. A variation for beginners is for A to play a little feeding shot after the boast to facilitate a drive and for B to feed a drive to the service box and then boast.
   (b) Defensive boast. A driving for length, B boasting. *Scoring.* With (b) score where A loses a point if he hits outside area 6 (or 8) (*see Fig 108*) and B loses a point if the ball is above the cut line or down.

3. *Boast, crosscourt/lob*
   (a) A crosscourts from the front court, B boasts from the back court.
   (b) A lobs from the front court, B boasts.
   Target area: crosscourts – side, floor, back; boasts – second bounce or first bounce in the nick.

4. *Circling*
   Straight length
   (a) Both A and B driving straight off the back wall. Lift the ball above the cut line and circle via the back wall to the half-court line and then the T. This allows the striker to move directly to the ball.
   (b) With volleys.
   (c) Con game: driving to area 6, volleying to 8.
   (d) Con game: driving to area 6, volleying to 8, dropping to 7.
   (e) Con game: driving to area 6, volleying to 8, volley dropping to 7.

5. *Boast, drop and drive*
   B boasts from the backcourt, A plays a drop shot and then a drive, B boasts and so on. As with all the exercises, if one of the shots is too tight put in a feeding shot and allow it to be continuous. This is a good exercise for practising an important combination.

6. *Two shots exercise*
   A drops and then crosscourts; B drives straight and then boasts.
   There are a number of exercises where one or both players can play more than one shot. A variation on the above exercise would be for B to straight volley and then boast.

7. *Alternating exercises*
   (a) Boasting and alternating straight and crosscourt drives. This is an exercise I use frequently to work on disguise. I first practised it with

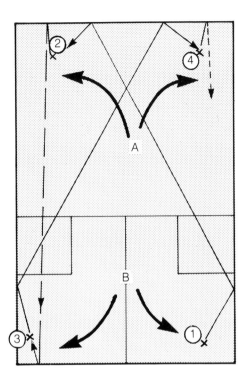

Fig 85   Boast and drive: A in the front court straight driving; B in the back court boasting. (1) B forehand boast; (2) A backhand straight drive; (3) B backhand boast; (4) A forehand straight drive and so on.

Vicki Cardwell just before her final British Open title at Derby. A alternates straight drives and crosscourts; B boasts.
   (b) Straight driving and alternating boasts and drops. A drives straight; B alternates boasts and drops.

8. *Diagonal and movement exercises*
   (a) Boast, drop, drive. A straight drives, B boasts, A straight drops, B straight drives, A boasts, etc.
   (b) Boast, drop, straight, straight. A boasts, B drops, A drives straight, B drives straight, A boasts, etc.
   (c) Crosscourt, straight volley, boast.

87

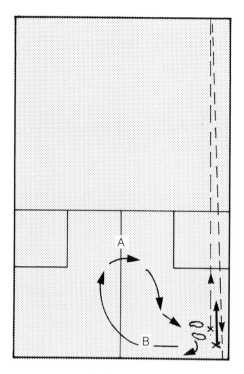

Fig 86   Circling: A and B straight driving and circling to recover the T via the half-court line.

A crosscourts, B straight volleys, A boasts, B crosscourts, A straight volleys, etc.

(d) Crosscourt, straight, straight, boast. A crosscourts, B drives straight, A drives straight, B boasts.

(e) Boast, drop, drop, straight, boast. A boasts, B drops, A drops, B drives straight, A boasts, etc.

9. *Volley exercises*

(a) Volleying across. On short line volley across court to each other and see how many shots you can play continuously.

(b) Con game. Player A has the right back half, B the left. They volley across to each other winning points when they land the ball in their opponent's area and lose points when they miss.

(c) A straight drives, B volley boasts.

(d) A crosscourts, B volleys straight and boasts own ball.

10. *Feeding exercises*

Feeding and the feeding progression

(a)

Fig 87   Circling: (a) Ross Norman straight drives from the back while Jansher waits on the T ready to move.
(b) Norman circles back to the middle while Jansher moves in to drive (*opposite above*).
(c) Jansher straight drives from the back and prepares to circle to the centre while Norman moves straight to the back to drive (*opposite below*).

(b)

(c)

kill and so on).

(b) B feeding from the front (straight or crosscourt) for A to play a shot short (straight or crosscourt drop, boast, etc.).

(c) A volley drops and drives, B behind feeds crosscourts.

11. *Circling and boasting*

(a) A and B play several straight drives and B boasts, A drives straight on the other side and they continue.

(b) Circling and crosscourts. As above with crosscourts. (Con game: straight drives to 6, crosscourts to 6 and volleys to 7, e.g. volley drops are allowed off the crosscourts.)

Threes and Fours Exercise

Pressure and variety can be provided with a number of exercises for three or four players. Here are a few examples.

1. *Boast and drive* One or two players in the front court straight driving with one each side in the back boasting in turn. The players boasting will have time to recover to the T and thus concentrate on their movement as well as their shots.

2. *Two players feeding* Two players feeding (short or long) from the back corners providing pressure for A to play a shot on (drive, volley or kill, etc.) each side. Use one or two balls.

are explained in more detail in the coaching section. I mention it here as the numerous feeding exercises can be a useful part of a pairs practice or squad session with each player taking a turn at feeding.

(a) B feeding from behind (straight or crosscourt) for A to play a shot back down the court (a drive, volley, lob,

89

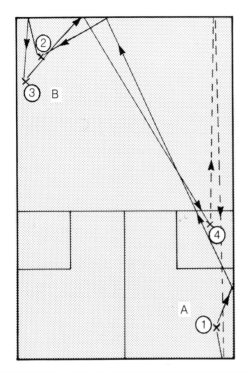

Fig 88   Two shots exercise: (1) A boasts; (2) B drops and then (3) B crosscourts; (4) A intercepts and volleys straight and boasts and so on (*left*).

Fig 89   Threes exercise. Two players feeding with two balls to apply pressure (*bottom left*).

3. *Rotating exercise* A crosscourts, B boasts, C waits on the T, C crosscourts, A boasts, B moves to the T, etc. (This can also be tried with four players.)

Two Pairs

The most economical practices from the court utilization point of view, and there-

Fig 90   Threes rotating exercise *(below)*.

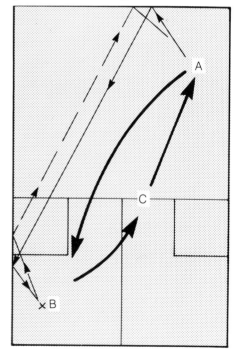

fore ideal in squads, is to use both sides of the court for straight pairs practices. These include circling and feeding exercises and condition games to various areas including the whole side.

Scoring

Competition focuses the concentration. First concentrate on grooving the shots. Cooperate with your partner and get into a rhythm. Once you have practised and got your shots right, then move to a competitive situation.

Adapt the scoring rules of your practice exercises and condition games to make them work. Here are some ideas to practise with.

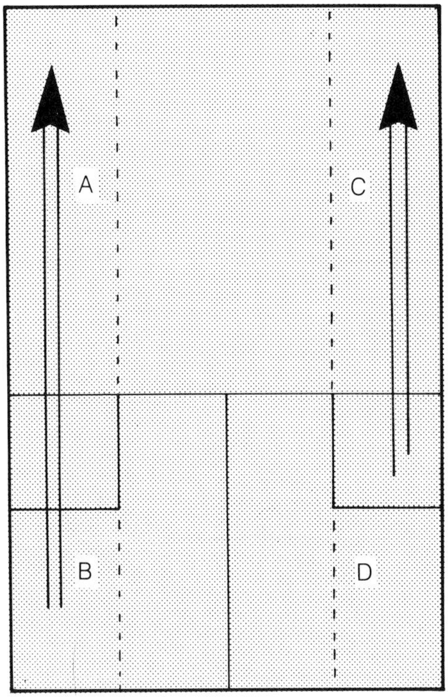

Fig 91 Two pairs: two players on each side of the court practising straight pairs exercises.

1. Serving (or just hitting off). The first shot has to be accepted for the rally to continue, i.e. you don't have to accept the serve.
2. Use American scoring (every point counts) to 6 or 9, 10, 15, etc.
3. Use handicaps: one player gets a start or one player is on normal scoring, one on American.
4. Use penalties. For example, if you play a particular shot or combination you lose a point, or if you hit the tin you lose two points.
5. Use bonuses, e.g. in the circling exercise if you hit the side wall behind the service box it is an automatic point.
6. Areas. Use chalk to mark out areas, for example, to extend or narrow the sidelines.
7. Tactical errors. A point is immediately lost if a tactical error is made.
8. Targets. Play a certain number of shots, to a set area. Who can get the best score?

BACK COURT GAME

Play a game just using the area behind the short line. You may play any shot in this area. A good rule to practise width is that a crosscourt must hit the side wall.

CONDITION GAMES

Condition games are the step between pairs practices and practice games.

The aim is to get systematic practice at particular aspects of your game, through repetition in a competitive game situation. It is a good way to become familiar with particular shots and tactics. Condition games are also a good way of providing close competition for players of different standards.

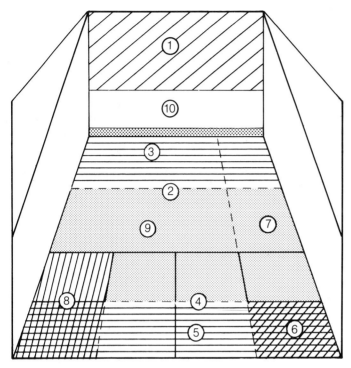

Fig 92   Practice areas

4. Back half – area behind short line.
5. Back quarter – area behind back of service boxes.
6. Back corners (left and right)) – within width of service box.
7. Sidelines (left and right) – within width of service box (or a chalk line). (This area can be gradually reduced depending on the standard of the player.)
8. Back half within sidelines (left and right) – behind short line and within the service box width.
9. Middle half – area between front quarter and back quarter.
10. Bottom half – front wall. Area below the cut line and above the tin.

The method is to place restrictions on either or both of the players. The restrictions can be in:

1. Area.
2. Placement.
3. Shots.
4. Combinations of shots.
5. Tactical rules.
6. Scoring.

Restriction Areas

1. Top half – area above the cut line.
2. Front half – area in front of short line.
3. Front quarter – area in front of a line approximately half-way between short line and front wall.

A condition game may be played where either any shot or restricted shots can be played to a particular area.

Placement

Additional restrictions can be applied.

1. Good length – all drives must bounce and hit the back wall (unless intercepted).
2. Good width – all crosscourts must hit the side wall before bouncing.

Shots

1. A good way to concentrate on a par-

ticular shot is to allow one or more defensive shots plus one or more attacking shots (by one or both players). For example:

(a) Player A and B – all shots to the back (restricted to an area 4, 5, 6 or 8) except drops.

(b) Player A – all shots to the back (restricted to an area e.g. 4, 5, 6 or 8) except, for example, volley drops and volley boasts or boasts, volleys, volley drops, volley boasts, or kills or any combination of these depending on the rules that you have set. Player B – normal game.

2. Of course the game could also be restricted just to particular defensive (back corner) shots, attacking (front corner) shots, or particular areas. For example:

(a) Players A and B. All shots to back half (area 4).

(b) Player A. All shots to front half only (a very attacking game – one of my favourites where you are playing a lot of shots and trying not to make mistakes). Player B. Normal game or restricted to areas 4, 5, 6, 7 or 8.

3. You can win the rally only with a particular shot. Win only with a straight drive, kill, drop, etc.

4. Hard and soft. A game of all hard shots or all soft.

Combinations

To develop a tactical awareness of particular combinations of shots you can make it a rule, that as a player, or even as a coach, which combinations must be played in a certain exercise or set of exercises (*see* Chapter 8).

Tactical Rules

One of the more unpleasant things I do when working on court with one of my pupils or when watching two of them play is to make tactical rules for them to play by. Conveniently I am often the person to make the absolute decision on their tactical indiscretions and stop the rally. A tactical error of a particular type will result in loss of a point. This may seem a little tough but for the coach it works well – you get instant results. A tactical error is where the player's decision to play a particular shot is wrong. Some of those which I use include:

1. Not returning to the T.
2. Playing short when your opponent is on the T.
3. Picking the wrong time for a shot.
4. Picking the wrong shot.
5. Hitting back to an opponent when you had the opportunity to hit away.
6. Not taking opportunities to volley.
7. Not taking opportunities to attack.

MAKE IT WORK

As a player or coach be flexible with rules and change them quickly if they are not appropriate.

PRACTICE GAMES

Not all your practice games should be played as competitive matches. Some of them will be though. This will be when you try to get all the parts of your game together and when you go for a result.

Practice games can also be used to practise particular parts of your game. This effort may be self-imposed or informal (as opposed to the formal rules of the condition game). You could work on a particular shot, combinations of shots, area, or type of game – hard driving, defensive, volleying, attacking. You may prolong the rallies to get the particular situation you want to practise.

The ideal partner for your practice games is someone with whom you could rally well but who would not put you under too much pressure.

PAIRS PRACTICE SESSION

Generally, try not to make your practice session a hotchpotch of odd exercises but work to a theme. before a competition, however, you may wish to run through a number of tried and tested exercises and get all your shots grooved in.

Here are some examples. Plan your own sequence using the practices and ideas outlined in this chapter. Don't arrive at the court and start scratching your head. Plan it and write it down beforehand.

SEQUENCE 1
1. Knock-up technique practice.
2. Length and crosscourts.
3. Boast and drive.
4. Boast and crosscourt.

5. Condition game to back half, crosscourts must hit the side.
6. Boast, drop and drive.
7. Volley boast and drive.
8. Condition game. Straight drive to area behind the service box plus boasting and volley boasting.

SEQUENCE 2
1. Knock-up technique practice.
2. Boast and drive.
3. Circling (driving).
4. Feeding for straight volley (twenty each).
5. Condition game, circling. Drive behind the service box and volley behind the short line. American scoring to nine.
6. Volleying across (on short line).
7. Volley game. Volleying across to back quarters. If you land the ball in your partner's square you win a point, if you miss the square you lose a point.
8. Condition game to back half, volleying as much as possible.

SEQUENCE 3
1. Knock-up technique practice.
2. Length and crosscourts.
3. Circling.
4. Game back half.
5. One or more pairs exercises on shots.
6. Game back half plus one (or more) short shots.

7

Coaching

LEARNING A SKILL

Research into 'motor skill acquisition' and theories of learning give us a little background into what a coach can do. Skills are learned by either imitating another person, consciously analysing the movement made, getting a 'feel' of the activity while performing, or by a combination of these methods.

A coach should use methods which will utilize these different paths to learning: demonstrating, explaining and doing.

'Unlearning' must often occur before progress can be made. During this phase 'retrogression' (a decrease in performance terms) can occur with resulting motivational problems. A coach must warn his pupil about too high an expectation of immediate results.

Learning takes place in spurts and plateaus. A coach helps to ensure that the plateaus are temporary, not permanent.

Learning a skill takes time. There are no short-cuts. Practice and patience are essential. Repetition is the key.

Practice must be done correctly for 'best' learning. A coach should spend some time watching, analysing, criticizing and helping his pupil practise.

Specific realistic goal setting gets results. Use the skills tests.

One effective and efficient method of teaching skills is the whole-part-whole approach. The learner first attempts the whole skill, then the various subskills and then integrates these into the whole skill again.

Individuals differ on how easily and by what method they learn different activities.

THE COACH

What I have learnt about coaching has been gained by trying to solve my pupils' problems on court. Attempt to do this and you will develop the knowledge and experience to get results from your pupils and the ability to adapt to their individual needs.

Develop a thorough knowledge of the game – its techniques, faults, shots, practices, skills and tactics. This book will help. Use the checks, check lists, guided instruction points and summaries.

Develop your own methods. Try things out. Learn to demonstrate each shot and technique clearly. Explain clearly, concisely and simply. Time yourself. Instruct using key points, check lists and summaries. Endeavour to make your points memorable.

Develop the ability to analyse. The first part of this is observation. Do not watch the ball, watch your pupil. What is he doing? The second is to study the parts. Watch his racket, feet, positioning in relation to the ball etc. The third is to work out the causes of problems. For example,

Fig 93   The author advises former British Champion Lucy Soutter between games.

learn to coach like this but pointers and a good run around are not going to develop the basic habits on which a player builds his game. Have the confidence to move from this and use both approaches.

Initially it will help you to plan your lessons and your series of sessions. Write down what you hope to do and the times for each activity. Be flexible. Endeavour to provide variety through a balance of activities but try to tie them into progressions or a theme rather than just a hotchpotch of activities.

The activities will include a knock-up assessment, assessment game, coaching exercises and drills (with and without ball), progressions, pressure exercises, solo practices, condition games and games implementing the theme.

One useful approach to lesson structure uses the *ideas* method.

Introduction Knock-up, discussion, assessment game.
Demonstration Select and demonstrate theme or activity.
Explain Explain and instruct.
Activities Work and activities starting easily and then increasing movement and difficulty progressively.
Summary Revise key points, set practices.

Course Structure

It is useful if a coach has an outline programme he can progress through while still being flexible enough to cater for pupils' individual needs. The individual

your pupil is missing the ball. Why? Is it ball control or is he not watching? Why is he looking up? Is he looking at the target area? Is he too close and leaning backwards? The fourth part is to use and develop methods to correct these problems.

Develop the ability to feed well. Are you giving your pupil the best chance to hit the ball and be successful?

Your manner can help your pupil's performance. Encourage and praise your pupil. Use a positive manner. Be receptive and encourage questions. Use 'positive reinforcement', enjoy it and do not talk.

Lesson Structure

There are two main approaches to coaching.
1. The 'basics' approach (practising the parts): learning, improving and practising the basic elements in your game (techniques, shots, combination, tactics) and then putting them together.
2. The game approach (practising the whole): playing a game. You may

lesson is a balance of activities, for example, fifteen minutes 'basics' and movement, fifteen minutes new shots and practices and ten minutes rules, games, tactics and programmes.

EXAMPLE BEGINNER'S COURSE
The following is an example of how to build up a beginner's basic course, with a specific 'topic' for each lesson.

1. Forehand *Activities*: Knock-up; forehand straight (coach single feeding); forehand moving from T; forehand solo practice.
2. Crosscourts and backhand *Activities*: knock-up; crosscourts; crosscourts from T; revise forehand; backhand straight; backhand from T; backhand solo practice.
3. Service and return of service *Activities*: knock-up; revise forehand and backhand; practise these together from T; service, service to T then driving exercise; demonstration of receiving position.
4. Drops: straight.
5. Volleys.
6. Lob.
7. Boast.
8. Crosscourt drops and reverse angles.
9. Back corners.
10. Shots and combinations.

Getting Started

WHAT DOES YOUR PUPIL WANT?
Discuss with your pupil what he feels his needs are. Are there specific problems? Does he want to learn the basics? Is it that he has hit a plateau and is not improving?

Ask him some questions. How long have you been playing? How often do you play? Are you in the Club leagues? Do you practise by yourself? What things do you want to do? What are your problems? Have you had coaching before?

WHAT DOES YOUR PUPIL NEED?
What a pupil perceives his problem to be and what his real needs are may be quite different. It is your job to assess his strengths (start here), weaknesses and limitations.

Analyse your pupil in the knock-up. Observe his footwork, positioning, balance, grip, swing etc. Check for faults.

Analyse your pupil in a short game. (I often use American scoring to six or nine.) Feed the ball to various parts of the court and make a mental list of points you want to make.

USE THE KNOCK-UP
Hitting across the court is a comfortable position for your pupil. Use it at the start of each lesson to let him settle down and to ease into the instruction situation. It is a good place to revise some basic ideas as you knock-up.

CREATE RIGHT LEARNING SITUATION
Do not be too eager to rush into instructions and correct all your pupil's faults at once. First create the right atmosphere in which your pupil is receptive and can feel successful, then move on from there. Go through these steps.

1. *Rapport* Introduce yourself and get to know the pupil.
2. *Relax* Give your pupil time to settle down and relax.
3. *Encourage* Everyone responds to encouragement. Praise your pupil at the start. Ignore nervous mistakes. Use 'good shot', 'well done', and 'it's going well'.

4. *Feed* It is your job as a coach to give your pupil the very best chance to hit the ball.
5. *Analyse*
6. *Instruct* Instruct in a step by step manner that will allow him to concentrate on one thing at a time. Often coaches provide more information than a pupil can use and just end up confusing him.

Basic Control

The first thing I look for in the knock-up situation is consistency of shot. If your pupil is still spraying the ball around the court and still making mistakes after the settling in period this is the first problem you must tackle.

Lack of control may be a co-ordination problem or a technical problem. A simple check on co-ordination is to ask a pupil to bounce the ball on his racket. If he has a problem with this then this is where you must start. (*See* Ball Control section.)

If the problem is a technique riddled with faults, work on this. Technique falls simply into three areas: movement control, racket control and timing. Many players rush their shots, get too close and off balance. The fault-finding section in Chapter 1 provides some ideas on solutions to these problems. Once pupils have slowed down, they are on balance and they are taking time for their shots, then they will be able to concentrate on the aspects of technique, movement, placement and tactics you have selected to practise and instruct on.

Now when your pupil is relaxed, encouraged, interested, has reasonable basic control, and is taking time for his shots, you are ready to move on with your lesson.

'Coaching Progression'

Gradually build up your routines. Don't be over-eager to rush into pressure exercises. It is what you are putting under pressure that is important. Work on control. Get consistency and accuracy, and endeavour to keep this while working through to movement and pressure.

You control the degree of movement and pressure by your feeding progressions (hand feed, single feed, continuous, alternate and random), your design of the routine and your instructions.

1. Practise without a ball. Groove the swing. Get a feel for the positioning, swing, stance and impact points.
   For example, stand your pupil on the extended half-court line and go through the stance and swing for the forehand straight drive. (*See* Practising Technique section in Chapter 1.)
2. Practise with the ball. Use feeding and solo practice routines, for example, feed the ball for your pupil and have him practise straight drives.
   Instruct on the shot and target area. (*See* Chapters 2, 3 and 5.)
3. Practise moving from the T and hitting. Use shadow practices as well as drills with the ball. For example, pupil moves from ready position on T, forward to straight drive and then recovers to T. (*See* Chapter 1, Court Movement.)
4. Practise anticipating, moving and hitting. For example, the coach feeds short and long. Pupil moves from T, forward and back depending on the feeds. (*See* Chapter 1, Court Movement.)
5. Practise under pressure. Gradually build pressure up with more difficult feeds, forcing pupil to come back to

the T (or play another shadow shot) and with quick volley feeds. For example, forehand straight drives from the T. Feed just above the tin and force your pupil to come back behind the short line each time. Do twenty shots to a target area. Only count shots that land in the area and movements that come completely behind the line (*See* Coaching Methods, Advanced Pressure Exercises.)

6. Practise anticipating, moving, selecting and hitting. Pupil selects the most appropriate shot from the range of choices set down by the coach. For example, forehand straight drives up and down the side, and the easy balls can be killed (or volleyed etc.). (*See* Combinations in Chapter 8 and Pairs Practice in Chapter 6.)

7. Practise in a game situation. Use a condition game that is designed for that particular shot or theme. For example, your pupil can only hit straight and to the back. (*See* Chapter 6 and Condition Games.)

Methods

FEEDING *(Fig 94)*

A coach spends a large amount of his time feeding balls for his pupil to hit. He will analyse the result in terms of technique and placement and comment and instruct on it.

The coach should provide a feed appropriate to the task he has set.

The feeding progression moves from hand feeding, single feeding, continuous feeding to pressure feeding.

Use a short swing with an open racket face. Initially lift the ball high and soft so it sits up and provides the ideal opportunity for your pupil.

INSTRUCTION

Instruction involves demonstrating, explaining and doing. Go through the technique or shot with the pupil. Get them to demonstrate it without the ball. Isolate and explain the various elements. Analyse and comment on their demonstration and go through it again together. Provide precise instruction, for example, 'stand on the line', 'point your toe directly at the side'.

AWARENESS

Use techniques and 'self checks' to show a pupil what he is doing. Try to make him aware of how this affects his control. When he has this 'feel' he can start modifying his behaviour.

Video is an invaluable aid as many

Fig 94 The art of feeding: the coach feeds and studies his pupil. Note the feed is high and soft. The pupil moves off quickly from his ready position on the T and starts preparing.

pupils do not have a good idea of what they are doing, when hitting.

TECHNIQUES

Controls Place strict controls on movement, time, swing and position. For example: Move when I hit! Take your racket back when the ball hits the wall! Do not go over the sidelines etc.

PREPARATION

Start your pupil in position and with the racket ready at an appropriate size swing.

FREEZE

Get your pupil to stop and freeze at the end of a shot and 'self check', for example, balance, distance, follow-through, grip or wrist. Call 'freeze' at various points in the stroke so you can show the pupil exactly what he is doing, at that point.

SELF CHECKS

Use the grip check, wobble check, feel and push checks.

ANALYSIS

Study the technique and faults sections.

REPETITION

Learning, changing and improving skills needs repetition. Get one thing right before moving on. Repeat the demonstration and the key teaching points.

STEP BY STEP

Provide appropriate size steps for your pupils' individual needs, that will allow them to be successful at each stage. Use the feeding and coaching progressions.

COMMENTARY

Provide 'positive reinforcement' during the exercises. Be specific. Do not just say 'good shot' but 'better balance', 'good preparation', 'good width' etc. Teach your pupil to be discriminating about his performance. Make clear and pertinent points. Ask for feedback. Keep your pupils 'on task' but do not overload them with information so they 'turn off'.

PRACTICE

Teach your pupil individual solo practices including the ball control exercises where appropriate. Use the skills tests. Provide targets.

GAMES

Use games and game type situations to teach positional play and tactics. For example have your pupil serve and come to the T. Feed a ball and ask him not to hit it. Discuss what would be the best shot. Play a game and stop if the wrong shot is played; 'You have hit it back to me'. Play a game and use the freeze check to see if your pupil is recovering the T.

ADVANCED PRESSURE EXERCISES

Pressure is applied by hitting the ball away from the pupil and using volley feeds to cut the time down.

1. The diagonal exercise. The coach is anchored in the back corner and feeds random boasts and straight drives for the pupil to hit crosscourts and straight drives.
2. Up and down. Coach feeding up and down one side.
3. Three corner exercise. The coach in the back corner feeds up and down and on the diagonal. This is my favourite exercise; it tests movement and change of direction forward and back as well as side to side.
4. Whole court. The coach is in the back and the pupil hits all straight drives

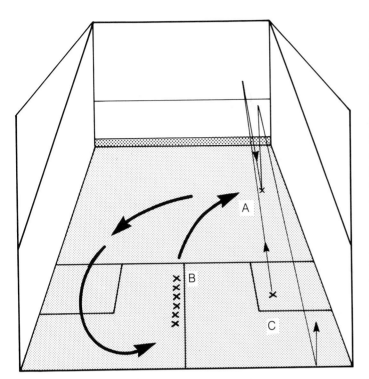

Fig 95   Group line routine: coach C feeds ball for pupil A to move from the T and drive straight. A circles around the back through the service box to join the back of the line while the coach feeds for B.

half-court line one behind the other with the front player (A) in a ready position. The coach feeds from behind the service box to the front court. Player A moves forward and plays the straight drive and recovers back through the service box to the back of the line. The coach feeds for player B and so on.

A number of shots can be practised with this routine, and shadow or movement work can be completed by the returning player.

GROUP TURN ROUTINES
Many single shot and individual exercises can be performed in a group situation.

Serving Player A in the service box with players B, C, D, E and F lined safely on the back wall. A serves, retrieves his ball, and proceeds to the back of the line. B then goes to the box for his turn.

Serving and Receiving Player A receives service and players B, C, D, E and F take turns serving while he practises receiving.

STATIONS
Several players, for example three each side, use the side wall for solo practice. Useful for ball control, technique and drop shot touch exercises.

PAIRS PRACTICE
See Chapter 6 for threes and fours double pairs exercises.

with the coach moving side to side as required and feeding randomly. This can also be performed from the front with the pupil dropping or boasting.

Group Coaching

Group coaching is not within the scope of this book except that I will introduce four routines that with a little imagination and organization can be adapted and used for a number of shots and situations.

GROUP LINE ROUTINE
(Fig 95)
A group of players (e.g. six) stand on the

101

8

Tactics

Squash is a physical battle of chess. It is about instant decision making. The decisions you make are tactical.

Squash is not a shot making sport, it is a rallying sport. The important thing when playing someone at your level is how well you fit the shots together.

You can improve your game by improving the parts of it (your shots, fitness etc.). You can also improve your game tactically by re-ordering the things you do, i.e. putting the parts together better.

So many different events are happening in a game of squash that it is often difficult to sort out the really crucial factors that decide whether a rally is won or lost. Where do the points really come from?

KEY AREAS

Let's look at the key areas. When you have a clear and realistic idea of why you are winning or losing, you will be in a better position to make tactical decisions about your game.

Court Coverage

The first thing you must do in a rally is get to the ball. The best players get to the ball better than anyone else and are very hard to beat. If you don't get to the ball you will lose the point. We look at this area in the court movement and the fitness sections.

Mistakes

When you have arrived at the ball, you must hit it safely. This seems self-evident, but most matches are won and lost on mistakes. This is a crucial area, and we have a special place for it.

Weak Shots

Don't congratulate your opponent if he slams the ball into the nick; work out where he played it from. It was probably your weak shot that gave him the chance. Here, we grasp one of the key ideas in squash: deprive your opponents of the opportunity to play winning shots. This is the defensive game.

Move your Opponent

Squash is a battle over territory; it is a positional game. The further you make your opponent run for a ball, the more unlikely he is to get it and the more likely you will win a point or force a weak ball. We look at this area in the positional game.

Apply Pressure

If your opponent doesn't have time to get to the ball because you have taken it early or hit it too hard for him, you will be winning points. We look at this area in the pressure game.

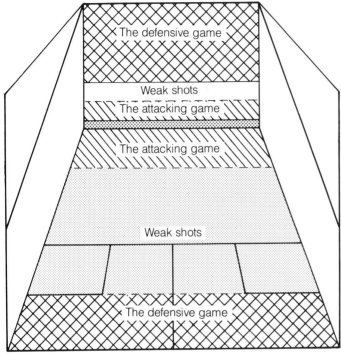

Fig 96   Simple tactics: use the height of the wall for your defensive (length) drives: don't hit too low when driving – it may be a weak shot.

Hitting Winners

It is easy to jump to the conclusion that whoever plays the most and best attacking shots is the winner. This, however, is often not the case. The idea of this list is to pinpoint the earlier crucial events before the final shot. Finishing the rally off and playing a winner is, of course, important and often crucial. We look at this area in the attacking game.

CHECK LIST

These ideas covering the key areas where points are won and lost in your game form the points check list.

1. Court coverage.
2. Mistakes.
3. Weak shots.
4. Moving your opponents.
5. Playing better shots.
6. Applying pressure.
7. Hitting winners.

ANALYSING MATCHES

Use this check list in deciding what are the really crucial events in each rally. From there, build up a total picture of the key areas where the match was won and lost. When analysing matches, ask the following questions:

1. Which player covered the court the best?
2. Which player made the most mistakes?
3. Which player played the most weak shots?
4. Which player made the other player move the most?
5. Which player played the better shots?
6. Which player applied the most pressure?
7. Which player hit the most winners?

MISTAKES

Squash matches are often won and lost on mistakes: the mistakes you need not have made (unforced errors) and the mistakes your opponent forced you to make (forced errors). Unforced errors are often the crucial area in winning and losing. If mistakes are a problem in your game, this section will help you sort out where and why you are making them. If you can then minimize them, you are well on your way to winning squash.

CAUSES

A mistake is a miss, a miss-hit, a shot that does not reach the front wall or a ball that is hit down or out of court. In looking at the causes behind these faults, we can examine four key problem areas:

1. Technical.
2. Tactical.
3. Temperamental.
4. Physical.

TECHNICAL AREA

1. *Mistiming* This is an ineffective connection of the moving racket with the moving ball by the moving player. It may be because of poor ball control, poor racket preparation or rushing.
2. *Taking your eye off the ball* This is the classic fault. If you are too close, off balance, or swinging your body, it is easy to move your head and take your eye off the ball. Don't look up at the target area, but keep your head forward, down and steady.
3. *Faults* Habitual failures to get good control over your movements and racket are faults (see faults section). These often result in errors.

TACTICAL AREA

1. *Attack the 'easy' ball* The easy ball is a weak shot payed by your opponent (e.g. one bouncing in the middle), that also gives you time to position, prepare and play your best shot. If you pick difficult balls to attack, you take a greater risk and overall will make more errors.
2. *Attack when your opponent is out of position* There is less chance that he

will get to the ball easily and therefore you can make the shot a little late.
3. *Allow for a margin of error* Strangely it never occurs to many players that the reason they hit the tin so often is because they aim an inch above it. Don't go for the ultimate shot every time. Aim high enough so that you don't make mistakes. Vary this depending on how difficult the ball is and how far from the front you are.

What is an acceptable level of mistakes? Out of ten drops, your opponent may, for example, get two or three back and win the rally. Your break-even point is not five but seven or eight. You must decide, but nine out of ten may be a reasonable target for your percentage error.

The seriousness of making an error will vary depending on the match situation. Don't take risks if match ball down, game ball down, or when receiving. When serving you cannot lose a point (only the service), so you can attack a little more and risk a little more.

TEMPERAMENTAL AREA

Nervousness and anxiety can account for errors from self-applied pressure through rushing, mistiming and stabbing at shots. Counter them with good mental and physical preparation, a 'playing in' period and 'returning to basics' as necessary.

Errors often go in little runs. This is a *lapse* and lapses cost you matches. Keep 'on task', *concentrate* and don't lose points through lapses.

Impatience is a major cause of errors. Wait for the right opportunity.

Discipline yourself. You cannot decide as each ball comes along what to do with it. You should have a game plan and general rules you break only occasionally.

PHYSICAL AREA

When you are tired and slower, you can easily lapse into mistakes. Don't be rash or attempt to finish the match with a string of lucky shots. Try to still 'pick' your shots and allow a greater margin of error.

ELEMENTS OF PLAY

Defensive Game

Squash is a simple game that is difficult to play well. How well you do the simple things will determine how well you play.

Defence is the key to winning squash. The player with the strongest basic game usually wins. The essential elements are length, width, recovering the T, watching, good court coverage, no mistakes and varying the pace.

The first battle in squash is for control of the T. You win this battle with a strong defensive or driving game. With the defensive game, you get the ball back safely and deprive your opponent of the opportunity to attack. With defence, you are not just negatively retrieving, but endeavouring to push your opponent out of position and force weak balls and mistakes. Defence is the base from which you attack at the right opportunity.

Pressure Game

Squash is a pressure game. Deprive your opponent of time so that he may not get to the ball; pressurize him into mistakes; make him scrape the ball up so his shots are weak, leaving you to kill the ball.

Apply pressure with volleys, kills, hard drives and by taking the ball early on the bounce before the side and the back.

Fig 97   The defensive game: a full length shot from Ross Norman has allowed him to take the T. Note that the tight shot he has played to the side may restrict his opponent to a straight drive which he can anticipate.

Fig 98   The pressure game: Australian Rodney Eyles applies pressure with the volley against Tristan Nancarrow.

105

VOLLEY

The volley should be a vital part of your game. Grind your opponent into the back then volley short. Move your opponent to the front and volley deep. Wait for the loose crosscourt shot and cut it off on the volley. Play a drop shot so tight that your opponent can only play down the wall where you can anticipate, move in and volley deep.

A volley will cut the time available to your opponent by half. Deprive your opponent of this time. Get volleying into your game.

HIT HARD

Hit the ball so hard it travels faster and gives your opponent less time to get to it. It will also be more difficult to hit.

Apply as much pressure through hard hitting as you can without sacrificing control. Use kills, hard low drives and dying length.

TAKE BALL EARLY

A squash ball slows down very considerably over its bounce and especially when it is rebounding off a wall. You deprive your opponent of time by taking it early on the bounce and before it reaches the side or the back.

Positional Game

Squash is a battle over territory. This territory is controlled from the T.

The further your opponent has to run, the more chance he has of not reach-ing the ball, missing it, making a mistake or playing a weak shot. This is squash as a positional game. The key idea is very simple – hit the ball away from your opponent.

When your opponent is in control of the T, you cannot hit the ball away from him and it is risky to attempt attacking shots. The first part of your game is defensive. Get your opponent off the T and out of position. Apply pressure to create the openings.

It is not necessarily the player with the best or the most powerful shots who is going to be successful but the player who can think while he is running, retrieving and recovering; the player who is cool and calculating, who is looking for and trying to create the opportunities to

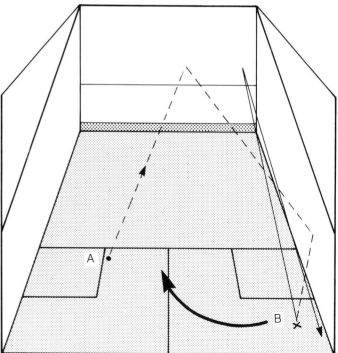

Fig 99 Combinations: straight return off the serve. With this combination, B places the ball away from A, puts him out of position and wins possession of the T.

move his opponent and attack. In other words, the player who can play the right shots at the right time.

The key ideas of positional play are simple:

1. Take your opportunities to hit the ball away from your opponent.
2. Hit the ball as far away from your opponent as possible.

You cannot work out the problems of positional play in a match, but a few general rules (that you may break occasionally) and specific ideas on which are the very best shots in a number of standard situations will help. I call these combinations.

GENERAL RULES

1. Don't play short when your opponent is on the T.
2. First get your opponent out of position in the back of the court. Then, when you have the right ball, move him to the front.
3. Only play short when your opponent is behind you.
4. Only play short if you can cover all your opponent's alternatives.
5. Hit the ball as far away from your opponent as possible.
6. Don't hit the ball back to your opponent and pretend you are wrong footing him.
7. Look for opportunities to move your opponent side to side and particularly up and down the court.

COMBINATIONS *(Figs 99–107)*

Combinations are your standard best replies in given situations. They give you the security of knowing you are playing the best shot.

1. *Return of serve*

Question What is the best standard reply to the serve?
Answer A straight length shot.

This shot is 'tight' all the way and on the opposite side of the court to the server. It will give the receiver the dominant position on the T and put the server out of position in the back corners.

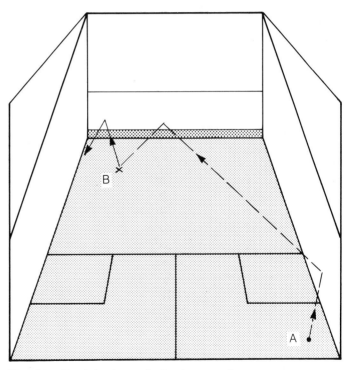

Fig 100 Straight drop of a back corner boast. Here B has taken the opportunity to move A the whole diagonal.

107

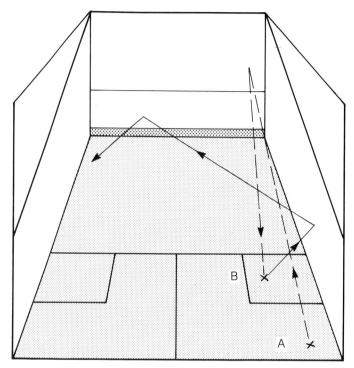

Fig 101   Boast the short straight ball. A's ball is short and B has seized the opportunity to move A on the diagonal with a boast.

2. *Drop of a back corner boast.* A classic attacking combination. Force your opponent to boast from the back with a good serve, crosscourt drive or lob.

Question What is the longest distance you can make someone run on a squash court?
Answer The diagonal. Remember this; use it in your positional play.

The best reply to the boast is the straight drop shot; the worst is the crosscourt shot.

3. *Boast the short straight ball.* If your opponent is out of position at the back of the court and you are on the T, his main reply should be a straight length so that he can win the T and put you out of position. If this is short of a length you have the opportunity to move him on the diagonal again; this time with the boast.

4. *Volley boast the 'loose' straight ball* If the straight drive from behind is loose, volley boast.

5. *Straight drop* the short crosscourt.

6. *Straight volley drop the loose crosscourt* Work out your own standard moves.

Combinations are not absolute rules but the best positional alternative. Use variations on these so that your positional play doesn't become predictable.

Attacking Game

Squash is as much about creating winning positions as it is about playing winning shots. When the situation presents itself, however, it is the player who can deliver the final stroke and finish the rally off who will win.

For simplicity, I refer to the front corner shots as the attacking game and back corner shots as the defensive game. Shots in between are often weak.

WHEN TO ATTACK
It is time to attack when you have two conditions:

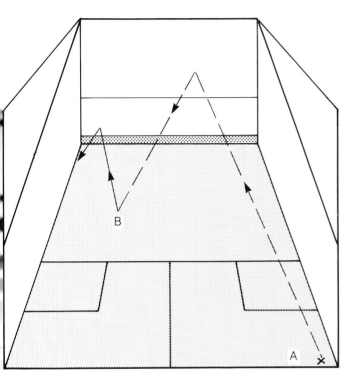

Fig 102   Straight volley drop the loose crosscourt. A's crosscourt has come through the middle and B uses the classic counter – a straight volley drop.

1. When you have an easy ball.
2. When your opponent is out of position.

Don't be afraid to attack when the opportunity presents itself. Don't go for a lucky shot. If you are successful, this lack of discipline will just encourage you to attempt more shots at the wrong time and will result in mistakes and easy balls for your opponent.

PLAYING WINNERS
There are a number of ingredients in playing a winner: touch, cut, speed, surprise, disguise, deception and variation. Placement can be to die (the ball bounces twice), to nick and to cling.

Develop a variety of shots, but practise them so that you can play them safely. You should refer to the mistakes section and the practice chapters. Don't play 'hit and miss' shots. Practise a shot and get it right then gradually work it into your game.

TACTICAL BALANCE

Squash is a 'thinking' as well as an action sport. The squash war involves mental, physical, shot making and tactical battles. If two competitors are evenly matched in the physical and shot making divisions, the tactics

Fig 103   Combination 5: Jahangir Khan plays a straight drop off a short crosscourt from Chris Dittmar.

109

Fig 104   Combination 6: The striker picks a loose crosscourt to intercept with a straight volley drop while his opponent is caught behind.

employed and the mental backing are crucial factors.

You can improve your game by improving at one of the modes of play: the defensive game, pressure game, positional game or attacking game. You can also improve your game tactically by playing the right shot at the right time; thinking in the right game mode while you are under pressure in a match.

Tactics are the *ideas* you use to *order* your game. Tactics are about getting the *right balance* between defence and attack, between positional play and pressure and between your hard and soft shots.

Some players are attacking players, some defensive, some emphasize hard driving, and some placement. Whatever

the emphasis, the balance between defence and attack must be maintained otherwise the tactical framework of the game collapses.

Percentage Squash

We started this chapter by saying that squash is instant decision making. Percentage squash is the overall result of the numerous small decisions you make. If the results are not right and if the percentages are not correct, you have to go back and look at the decisions you are making.

If each time you played a shot you had to stop and assess the chances of fulfilling your aims, your game might be less rash

Fig 105 Qamar Zaman, one of the great attacking players of all time, attacks from deep while his opponent, the eight times British Open Champion Geoff Hunt, is on the T. Will he get the ball?

Fig 106 Combination 2: drop off a back corner boast. The player in the back corner has been forced to boast. His opponent takes advantage of this by playing a straight drop.

and more calculated and disciplined. In addition, If you had to decide what your score out of ten attempts at a shot was likely to be, would you select the one you have?

Your game should not be grudgingly negative and, of course, you can use surprise, disguise, deception and variation, but you must be aware of the overall results.

Your game should follow a pattern.

Fig 107 Combination 3: boast the short straight ball. The mid-court player seizes on a straight ball that has landed short of a length to move his opponent over the diagonal to the furthest corner.

Game Plan

Develop a flexible structure for your game that suits your attributes, so you know exactly what you are trying to do.

Start your game with defence to establish consistency and win the T. Try to keep this throughout the match and apply and relieve pressure as necessary. Force openings and take opportunities. Continually move in and out of your defensive game and into your attacking game.

Your Opponent

Your game plan is flexible as it will vary depending on your opponent. Ideally,

you will already have been able to study your opponent, and if not, the first part of your match will involve assessing him and adapting your game to the threats and the opportunities.

If your opponent is excellent at hard driving, do not try and out hit him but vary the pace and play tight. If he is good at volleying, then you need excellent width, more straight shots, no loose crosscourt shots and harder, lower drives. If he is good at defence, you must try and match him but still play positively, take opportunities and move him. If he is very fit, you must take your opportunities and not try to prolong the match. If his fitness is susceptible you can prolong the rallies, maintain the pressure and endeavour to move him. If he is slow, use surprise shots and interceptions. If he is fast he may move too quickly. Use delay and deception and give yourself time by varying the pace.

Play the game at your pace not at that of your opponent. The superior tactical player controls the pace of the match and the type of game. Impose your game on your opponent.

Changing Your Game

The rules are very simple. Firstly *don't* change a winning game. You have the tactical balance right for your opponent. Don't spoil it, you may not be able to get it back.

Secondly, *do* change a losing game.

1. Change the tactical balance. If you are 'loose' or making errors or pressurized, it will mean 'back to basics', i.e. more defence. If you are rallying comfortably but not winning points, you may need to play more attacking shots or exert more pressure.

2. Change the pace, placement or the type of shots you are using. This is why you try to develop a number of tactical possibilities in your practice games. You then have alternative tactical options which you can test on your opponents as you search for weaknesses to attack.

Match Preparation

Develop a routine that suits you so that when the match starts you are ready technically (having grooved your shots beforehand and during the knock-up), physically (having completely and thoroughly warmed up), mentally (having 'psyched-up' before coming on to court and 'tuned-in' during the knock-up), and tactically (having checked off the key elements in your knock-up check list).

KNOCK-UP CHECK LIST

1. Time. Take time for your shots.
2. Width. Hit the side wall on the cross-courts.
3. Length. Make the ball bounce and then come off the back. Play a few straight drives for good length.
4. Vary the pace. Play a few lobs and straight lobs.
5. Volley. Feed a few balls to yourself if necessary and volley.
6. Drop shots. Play a few drop shots to yourself, perhaps after your opponent has boasted. Allow a margin 'for error'.

Get these shots and ideas working in your knock-up, so that when the match starts they are well-oiled and ready to use.

TACTICAL SUMMARY

1. Use the points check list to find out where you are winning and losing.
2. Don't make *mistakes*. Work out which areas you are making them in and try to eliminate them.
3. Use the *defensive game* to win the T. Force your opponent into the back corners with good length and width.
4. Use the *pressure game* to force openings. Volley, hit hard and take the ball early.
5. Use the *positional game* to move your opponent. Learn the rules of positional play and the standard combinations.
6. Use the *attacking game* to finish the rallies.
7. Tactics are the balance between your defensive and attacking games and between your hard and soft shots.
8. Think in terms of the overall effect of your play (in percentage terms), not in terms of isolated events.
9. Plan your matches.
10. Prepare mentally, physically, technically and tactically for your matches.
11. Impose your game on your opponent.
12. Attack your opponent's weaknesses.
13. Don't change a winning game.
14. Do change a losing game.
15. Attack when you are serving – you cannot lose a point.
16. Defend when you are receiving – you can lose a point.

113

9

Temperament

Squash is a mental battle. It is a competitive and combative confrontation in which you assert yourself over your opponent. It is also a battle with yourself to control 'nerves', to concentrate and to come up with a 'performance'.

We see the mental battle clearly in the drama of the fightback. The determination, concentration and sometimes pain as all resources are mobilized. Geoff Hunt was beaten to a walk in the classic British Open Final with Jahangir Khan in 1981. Then came one of the great fightbacks in squash history as the champion, staring defeat in the face, after two hours of combat slowly and coolly pulled his game together and collected point after point to finally draw level and then pass his opponent.

The champion's temperament allows him to play near his best consistently. For other players their performances can fluctuate. To the player the reasons are simply rationalized, for example, 'my forehand just wasn't working' may mean 'I just had an argument with my wife before the match'. Outside pressures and worries of everyday life affect performance. Good match preparation can help to rectify this.

Some players seem to have impressive ingredients in skills and fitness but don't get it together in a game. They are not thinking in the clear and simple terms necessary for success in squash.

Often players perform well in practice games but fail to achieve their best in competition. They may succumb to 'pre-match tension', 'nerves' or 'fright'. Relaxation and anxiety management techniques can help them.

Others seem to have poor ingredients but get the 'performance'. They are good performers and will rank high in concentration, patience, determination, fight, aggression and calculation.

Poor competitors can 'go off' and even 'crack' in a match. They lose patience, lapse, 'give in', make excuses, worry, become distracted, frustrated and even lose their temper. Your mental performance will need to be related to your personality. Your temperament, however, is not something fixed and unchangeable but, like your ideas and attitudes, it can change. You can develop your mental skills to cope better with competitive situations. Be critical of your mental performance. Understand your make-up, your strengths and weaknesses and work on them.

Work on the positive factors you need: concentration, patience, determination, alertness, aggression, calculation, coolness, fight, belief, confidence and being 'psyched up'.

Recognize, avoid and learn to cope with the negative factors: frustration, nervousness, anxiety, choking, freezing, staleness, dejection, lapses and being 'over psyched'.

Arousal Curve *(Fig 108)*

Some nerves are not a bad thing. To get your best performance you need to be attentive and a little keyed-up. Being too casual, not 'psyched up', inattentive or 'not really being there' will result in a poor performance. Being very anxious, over-tense or excited, over-psyched and over-aggressive won't allow you to think simply and clearly and will detract from your performance.

The arousal curve helps us to see the importance of the balance between these two extremes. The more aroused you get, the better the performance until a point when you are too aroused and performance decreases. Try to manage your arousal level to get the best performance.

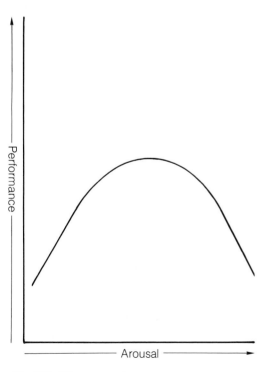

Fig 108   The arousal curve.

Anxiety

Competitive squash is a very stressful situation. It can result in anxiety or nerves which can vary from a slightly nervous excitement which disappears as the match progresses to feelings of increasing apprehension in which the body doesn't seem to obey you properly and you find it extremely difficult to concentrate. It may result in 'butterflies', a 'racing' heart, sweaty palms, a dry mouth, and a feeling of being physically sick. This type of excess anxiety will affect your ability to perform. Like the champion, you can learn to control it.

Learning to relax physically will help you control the physical responses you feel when you are anxious and tense. Progressive relaxation where you tense a muscle group, holding it and then relaxing it, will help. Start at your toes and work through the body. This is a technique you can use in the build-up to competition but not immediately before.

Short-circuit negative thoughts and worry by supplanting them with positive 'coping' thoughts which will help and not hinder your game.

Think positively, act as if you will be successful and try to look forward to the match. Plan some positive thoughts or images to use in your match if worry strikes. Slow down and create time to gain composure. Try not to rush.

Techniques to help control anxiety:

- Put yourself in relaxing pre-match situations.
- Prepare for your match (*see* Match Preparation).
- Use audio tapes of relaxing music or perhaps inspirational messages.

115

Fig 109 Eight times British Open champion Susan Devoy set herself apart from the other players with her determination. Here concentrating fiercely she applies the pressure to Sue Wright.

Concentration

Squash thinking is the ability to concentrate on simple ideas. Don't make it too complex. Don't let your concentration wander or be distracted. How well you play depends on how well you think.

Empty your mind before the start of a match. Take out all external and distracting ideas. Pick one simple thing to concentrate on. Try to focus all your attention on the ball for a period.

Your mental performance concerns your ability to keep on concentrating throughout the match. Monitor your own performance. Use key ideas: 'Have I got the T?', 'Am I forcing him to take it off the back?' and so on.

A *lapse* is when concentration drifts. If you examine a score-sheet you will see there are often tight groups of service changes and then runs of points. These runs are often the lapses that cost your matches. Watch out that a mistake does not result in a lapse of concentration and a run of points against you. Be aware of the danger areas.

DANGER AREAS

Match or game ball up, or after a good lead. Don't relax – it is not won yet. Keep the pressure up.

After a mistake, tactical error, bad decision or after losing a long rally. Don't let your disappointment or anger affect your concentration.

Crowd distraction, a break (e.g. broken ball), opponent's distracting and delaying tactics, non arrival of support. Block out all distractions.

Concentrate on the next point. Don't let

- Learn to relax physically.
- Practise deep breathing, inhaling slowly through your nose, holding in the stomach and exhaling slowly through your mouth.
- Practise thought stopping. When a negative thought occurs use a trigger like shouting 'stop' aloud or internally to stop it.
- Substitute positive thoughts for negative ones.
- Set achievable and positive goals.
- Use imagery. Imagine yourself playing well.

116

unpleasant past events in the game affect your performance. Don't brood on bad decisions, disappointing games and unlucky shots. Clear your head for the point coming up.

Match Preparation

How well you start your match is down to planning and the pre-match routine you establish. Develop a routine of your own; it will give you security. Go through these steps:

1. *Organization* Make sure you are in plenty of time and have all the equipment and back-up equipment necessary.

2. *Warm-up* Use a warm-up routine. Warm-up, loosen-up, stretch and groove.

3. *Mental preparation* Find out what works for you. Try finding a little place by yourself for a few minutes.
   (a) Relax and empty your head.
   (b) Concentrate on something simple.
   (c) Mental practice; rehearsal. Run through some shots in your head.
   (d) Preview your tactics. Run through the knock-up check list and game plan in your head.
   (e) 'Psych-up'; become a little aggressive.

4. *Use the knock-up check list.*

117

10

Fitness

You may well be one of the many players who took up squash to help you get fit. Now, having been bitten by the bug and perhaps playing the game more frequently and more competitively, you will realize that actually you need to be fit to play winning squash. It is important to be realistic here, because no matter how fit you get, the skill, tactical and mental elements of the game will remain key factors in your success. However, if you can improve your fitness, it may well give you the edge in a tight match, as well as allowing you to survive longer and learn when playing better and more experienced players.

When people talk about fitness, one almost immediately pictures the marathon runner, or a player who endures long rallies while barely drawing breath. It is more often than not the endurance factor that people consider. However, the general term fitness covers a variety of fitness elements that will contribute to physical performance. Endurance is just one of these. An Olympic sprint champion would struggle to run a marathon at a decent pace, but there are few that would argue that he is not fit; so the element of specificity comes into play – you need to be fit for the demands of your sport, especially a sport such as squash which can reach a high level of intensity in a short period of time.

FITNESS DEMANDS OF SQUASH

One of the difficulties of trying to establish the physical and physiological demands of squash is that there is no set duration or intensity in a match. Two players could be playing for as little as 30 minutes one day, but require over an hour to determine the winner on another day. Similarly, because styles of play can vary, the pace and intensity can change from match to match. To build a picture of the fitness demands of squash, sports scientists have monitored players' physiological responses, such as their heart rate throughout matches, as well as examined the fitness attributes of players of different standards.

Aerobic Endurance

The heart rates chart taken during a typical match (Fig 110) reveals that a player's heart rate will rise rapidly at the start of a match and will remain elevated throughout the duration of the contest. In between games there is a sufficient pause for the heart rate to drop, but there is only 7 seconds in between rallies, which gives little scope for recovery. This shows that squash is a taxing game and it is easy to see why it is an attractive option for someone wishing to get fit. Blood samples taken during competitive and simulated matches have revealed relatively low lactate concentrations. This indicates that the overall nature of the game is predominantly aerobic. This means that in the main, the body is able to take in and utilize sufficient oxygen to fuel the muscular activity whilst play is in progress. As the heart rate is usually above 80 per cent of maximum for the duration of the match (which is usually at the very least 30 minutes) there is a great requirement for aerobic endurance. As your aerobic endurance improves, you will be able to maintain a higher intensity of exercise for longer periods and your heat tolerance will also improve. You will also recover better in between rallies and games. Aerobic fitness is a key fitness ingredient for squash, so part of your training must address this.

Anaerobic Endurance

In gruelling rallies where your opponent has you under pressure and running relentlessly from corner to corner, a different component of fitness comes into play. When such supramaximal bursts come into play, you will incur a temporary oxygen deficit. This means that because you cannot immediately take in sufficient oxygen to match that required for this high rate work, the body uses a different energy system to fuel the muscles. When you have finished the rally and are left standing there panting, your current demands for oxygen are low (because the work has stopped) but you are still grabbing in oxygen to pay off the oxygen debt remaining from the rally.

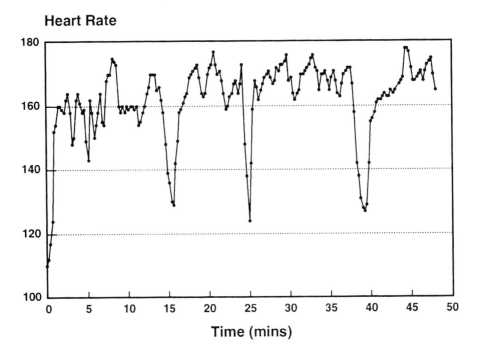

Heart Rate

Fig 110   Heart rate chart during a typical squash match.

The ability to keep going in these particularly fatiguing conditions are also quite trainable and form another vital aspect of squash match fitness. This anaerobic endurance can be developed either on or off court.

Strength and Power

You might think that strength and power should be left to the body builder, but they are both important fitness attributes for squash. You may consider too that strength is required in the playing arm to help up the pace of your killing drives; but such pace is better developed by improving skill and timing, rather than by simply pumping iron. The main strength requirement for squash is in the muscles of location and posture. The legs are involved in lots of bending and braking activity (eccentric contractions) which are particularly tiring and liable to cause stiffness for a few days if you have not played for a while. Solid toning and conditioning is also required for the back and abdominal muscles, a much neglected area in most fitness routines. Although the grip strength of the playing hand is found to be greater in good players, it is of little use working on grip strength in the weights room. This strength will improve as you play more squash. A training effect is very specific to the stimulus that causes it.

Power is a combination of both force and velocity and is thus very important to help improve your pace off the mark. Leg power will also help you push back from shots and help you recover the T before your opponent has played the ball, recover all but real winning shots and get to the ball early enough to deprive your opponent of time and apply pressure.

Speed

Speed around the court is essential if you are going to be competitive in your matches. This aspect of fitness, however, is primarily a function of the above sections. If your leg power is sufficient and both anaerobic and aerobic endurance can maintain it, then you should be in good shape to maintain speed around the court. Squash speed, however, also involves co-ordination. Speed is as much about neuro-muscular development as about physiological conditioning. You need to train the ability to move your feet quickly in the right pattern, often changing direction, which involves agility. To improve speed around court, you must perform drills aimed at increasing the skill of moving your feet quickly.

Mobility and Flexibility

These underrated, yet vital, aspects of fitness should be practised regularly both to increase the range of movement of the musculature about their joints and to help prevent injury. Stretching should be performed as part of the warm-up and cool-down processes, to help prepare for your performance and try to limit future muscle stiffness and soreness. An increase in range of movement in the back and shoulder region, as well as in the legs, can improve efficiency of movement on court and thus enhance your performance. In your programme you should consider both static stretching (which works on the elastic component of the muscle) and dynamic and PNF (proprioceptive neuromuscular facilitation) stretching which works more on the stretch reflex. Examples of these follow in the chapter.

HOW TO TRAIN FOR FITNESS

Whatever type of fitness training you decide to perform, there are a few general principles that need consideration: for example, from time to time, there must be an element of progression in the training that you do. Simply running for twenty minutes at the same speed, three times per week, will do little to change your fitness after a few weeks. You need to add extra stimulus, or *overload*, in order to challenge the body further and make it adapt to a new training level. Remember the actual training effect does not take place while you are running, but during the interim periods between exercise sessions. Rest, therefore, is a vital component of your training process and should be included thoughtfully within the schedule.

You can advance your training through a variety of options. Increasing the *frequency* of training within your schedule is one such method. Instead of running just once a week, building up to two, three or four sessions per week gradually is a sound means of progression. Similarly, the *duration* of sessions can be lengthened to boost the training stimulus. Both of these methods can combine to increase the overall *volume* of training that you perform.

Altering the intensity of your fitness work is another effective method of progressing. This may mean that you run quicker, perform more press-ups in a set time, use a higher step in a step aerobics class, or use a greater resistance in the weights room. Anything that makes the work you do harder is a valid means of increasing intensity.

To increase your fitness, the overload needs to be significant and regular. However, if you simply want to maintain your fitness, you can drop the amount of work that you do. Most research indicates that it is better to drop the volume, but keep the intensity for maintenance. If you do drop training for a while, whether it be for a break or holiday, injury or illness, you will start to lose some of the fitness you have gained. This is because training effects are reversible. The message here is definitely use it or lose it!

It is important that you get into the habit of warming up and cooling down properly, both before and after exercise – whether on or off court. Adequate warm-up involves an element of pulse raising for at least 10 minutes, which is best achieved by gentle whole body exercise, such as jogging, skipping or cycling. This should be followed by relevant stretches selected from the collection shown later. All this should be done before picking up the racket. After playing or training a similar process should involve a gentle jog followed by some stretching of the relevant muscles.

Specific Training

It is important to remember that work you perform on court whilst playing and practising is still physical training in its own right. In fact, it is the most specific type of training that you can do. Practice matches and pressure drills on court with racket and ball are a good way of working on the fitness requirements of squash and should be encouraged as a means of boosting match fitness. Similarly ghosting sessions, with the racket in hand, are also important to help improve speed and movement around the court. It is important to decide carefully what you wish to achieve from the session before

GHOSTING

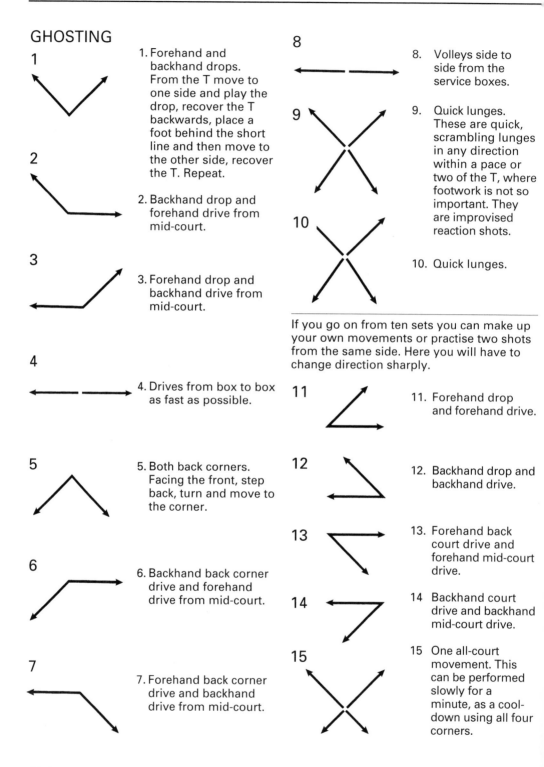

1

1. Forehand and backhand drops. From the T move to one side and play the drop, recover the T backwards, place a foot behind the short line and then move to the other side, recover the T. Repeat.

2

2. Backhand drop and forehand drive from mid-court.

3

3. Forehand drop and backhand drive from mid-court.

4

4. Drives from box to box as fast as possible.

5

5. Both back corners. Facing the front, step back, turn and move to the corner.

6

6. Backhand back corner drive and forehand drive from mid-court.

7

7. Forehand back corner drive and backhand drive from mid-court.

8

8. Volleys side to side from the service boxes.

9

9. Quick lunges. These are quick, scrambling lunges in any direction within a pace or two of the T, where footwork is not so important. They are improvised reaction shots.

10

10. Quick lunges.

If you go on from ten sets you can make up your own movements or practise two shots from the same side. Here you will have to change direction sharply.

11

11. Forehand drop and forehand drive.

12

12. Backhand drop and backhand drive.

13

13. Forehand back court drive and forehand mid-court drive.

14

14 Backhand court drive and backhand mid-court drive.

15

15 One all-court movement. This can be performed slowly for a minute, as a cool-down using all four corners.

you start and keep that goal in mind. If you want to work on aerobic endurance, a match will help, but this fitness aspect is best developed off court.

For anaerobic endurance, you can either work specifically on court, or off court. On-court practice drills, combining skills and fitness, are effective. Here the intensity of work must be hard and work bouts should last between 15 and 45 seconds. To keep the intensity high, allow yourself short recovery periods between repetitions, but avoid letting these last longer than 30 seconds. The drills can be performed with or without a ball, but should involve running from the T to the corners in a manner that you would use in a game, until your set time period has elapsed. It makes sense to alter the order of the corners you run to (having a partner randomly calling them helps). To progress over a number of weeks, you can either build up the time that you are working for during each repetition (starting at 15 seconds and building up to 45 seconds), or you can build up the number of repetitions, to expand the volume. You can also split the reps into sets, for example, three batches of eight reps, allowing a longer recovery of 90–120 seconds at the end of a set, and start to add extra sets of reps. If you want to increase the intensity, simply try to increase the amount of ground you cover in your exercise time periods.

To increase speed around the court, you can use a similar procedure, but the work periods should be less than 10 seconds long and the recovery periods at least 45 seconds. Although you can increase the volume of work for this session by adding reps and sets, it is important to remember that the key variable here is the intensity, so concentration should be on working more quickly, rather than simply building volume.

Non-Specific Training

AEROBIC ENDURANCE
There is no shortage of options for training to increase aerobic endurance. The simplest and most accessible is running, which is the preferred option as it is most specific to squash. This mode of activity has the advantage of the fact that you can nip out of your front door at any time and get on with it. Progression is easy using any of the methods discussed above, but get in the habit of running for time rather than distance. The duration should normally be at least 30 minutes to be of real benefit.

If you have not done much exercise in a while, you will have to build up to this, starting from as little as five minutes at a time and adding a couple of minutes each week. As it is aerobic endurance you are training, it is important to keep the intensity hard, but comfortable. You should be able to talk, so running with a friend or partner can keep a check on this, as well as to alleviate some of the boredom. Running on soft surfaces such as grass or a treadmill is advisable to reduce the risk of injury.

As running is not everyone's cup of tea, other modes of activity are often used. Cycling and swimming are excellent ways of developing cardio-respiratory fitness, but will not give the peripheral adaptations in the correct musculature like running does. With the boom in health and fitness at most clubs, there is the opportunity to workout in a gym. Treadmills and bikes can be used while stepping and stair machines are quite effective means of developing aerobic fitness. You should progress in exactly the same manner as that suggested above for running.

High-impact and step aerobics sessions are also suitable alternatives as they will keep the heart rate at a sustained level, like that in squash, and also have the benefit of strengthening the leg muscles, often eccentrically as well as concentrically. Such classes may be useful, as they can be quite fun and motivating, and may also help encourage you to keep to a routine – a vital aspect of any training schedule.

Another mode of activity, which you can perform almost anywhere, is skipping, which is popular with squash players as it also helps with co-ordination and the development of speed. Skipping is a valid method of aerobic conditioning, provided that the intensity and duration are appropriate, but be careful not to skip on too hard a surface.

ANAEROBIC ENDURANCE

The goal of these sessions is to increase local muscular endurance in the legs and, due to their fatiguing nature, are often the most taxing sessions. To get most benefit from such training, it is advisable to take an easy day after an anaerobic session and certainly avoid performing such work the day before a match! If you are doing anaerobic training away from the court, you must remember the principles mentioned in the section on specific training. The emphasis should be on high intensity work performed in repetitions lasting 15–45 seconds, interspersed with only short recovery periods. This can be done in a park and is most effective if performed in shuttle form, using a distance of about 33ft (10m). This means you will be turning and changing direction as well as accelerating,

the most tiring aspect of performance, many times. Another option is to perform short hard efforts up a hill, to increase the intensity, followed by a quick jog back down before repeating. The problem here is keeping the recovery time down, so it is best to keep the hill runs to no more than 20 seconds.

Performing short hard reps on the machines in the gym is another option, but not particularly favoured, because the idea is to condition the muscles pertinent to squash. Although cycling works on the leg muscles, this activity does not recruit the correct muscle fibres in the same way. For anaerobic endurance, specificity is really the key principle. Skipping can be used as an alternative, but you have to be quite skilled to reach the intensity required for the session.

Local muscular endurance can be trained with circuit training, where a variety of conditioning exercises are used in succession to form a hard training session. Here the emphasis is upon performing a lot of exercises at a high rate, with little recovery, thus the session is quite different from that used to develop strength and power. From the nine anaerobic endurance exercises in the next section select six to make an anaerobic conditioning circuit. This circuit emphasizes the lower body which makes sure that the same muscle groups are hit again and again, rather than alternating between upper and lower body – a more appropriate mixture for aerobic conditioning.

Start by performing ten reps of each exercise in succession to form one circuit. You can then progress by adding reps or sets of reps. You should keep the speed of exercises high to make sure the intensity is good. Performing such exercises against the clock may appear a sound method of maintaining and monitoring high intensity, but usually results in poor technique and associated injury risk. Thus building on the number of exercises is the preferred method. It also makes sense to alter the exercises used and the order in which you perform them. This helps to avoid the problem of starting to get very good at one type of circuit training without significantly improving your fitness for squash – never lose sight of why you are doing the training in the first place!

STRENGTH AND POWER

As the emphasis here is upon developing pure strength and power, the number of repetitions is usually low. This allows the quality of the work to be very high and thus effective to cause an increase in strength. If too many reps and sets are used, the quality of your workout will deteriorate and the session will drift more towards anaerobic endurance than increasing pure strength. With this high intensity in mind, it is more common to perform strength workouts with equipment in the gym. However, some of your work can be done at home, because not all strength work requires weights. A good example of this is when working upon the muscles of posture. As these do not directly affect the performance of the game, they are notoriously neglected by many players. The specific muscles in question are those in the lower back and abdominal region, as well as the gluteals (buttock muscles) and hamstrings. Strength in these muscles of posture is essential for almost any sport as they help keep form when under the duress of fatigue.

In training these muscles an element of toning is more appropriate than trying to grow huge muscles. The no-rush circuit is a series of exercises designed to work on these muscles in a safe, controlled manner. As the name suggests there is no time limit in the no-rush circuit, in which a series of exercises are performed consecutively to form a set. Start with ten reps of each exercise. For progression, simply add to the number of reps in each set over successive weeks until you can do twenty reps; then drop the number of reps down to ten and add to the number of sets and so on.

Other circuit type exercises can be performed at home to contribute a little to strength and more to power, as they work on quick movement with resistance. However, more effective strength and power gains will result from training with weights in a gym. When you train in a gym, you will be faced with two options – to use free weights or machines. Free weights are the preferred option for a player with a little experience in weight training who trains with others. These training partners can then act as spotters, who watch the lifter and are ready to catch the weights if need be. If you are inexperienced, or train alone in the gym, you should opt for machines, which are a little safer and do not require spotters.

A whole variety of training methods exist for weight training, but once again it is important to bear in mind that you are training to be a better squash player, rather than to be an Olympic weight-lifter or the star in an action movie! With this is mind, your aim should not instantly be to lift the whole stack of weights available, or perform every type of exercise that you see. Careful selection of exercises is important and should contain a balanced mixture of both lower and upper body exercises. The exercises that you can perform will partly be governed by the equipment that is available in your gym, but a few principles should be adhered to.

Always start with compound exercises, those which use a variety of muscle groups in the action, such as bench press, squat or power clean. You can then move onto isolation exercises afterwards, which work specifically on one muscle group. It is also important to work on pairs of muscles to avoid gaining imbalances. For example, if you work on the biceps, your routine should also work on the triceps; or if you work on the quads (thigh muscles) you should also work on the hamstrings (back of the thigh).

Putting together the schedule takes getting used to, but starting with the compound exercises is a safe start, as these are more whole body exercises. The bigger problem is usually how much weight to use and how many sets to perform.

The style and type of training very much depends upon the training effect required. To work on pure strength you must have a very high resistance, so the amount of reps should be low. You should perform two to four of just four or five reps in a slow controlled manner and the resistance should be as much as you can manage safely for this. The recovery should be sufficient in between sets, so 2–3 minutes will be the minimum; this means that you should be prepared to spend a reasonable time in the weights room. The main angle of progression will be to lift heavier weights as this will improve your strength.

For development of power, which should take place only after a basic strength foundation has been built over several months, a slightly lower resistance should be used, but the speed of movement a little faster and four to eight sets is more appropriate.

If you want to work on your strength endurance, you would use a much lighter weight and perform lots of reps. However, this can be done with your own body weight at home and is more like the anaerobic endurance circuits above.

SPEED

Speed is a combination of power and co-ordination. The power will be developed by the methods described above. Speed of movement is also developed by performing circuit training exercises quickly followed by long rest intervals. Again body weight is the best resistance to use here, as a low resistance will allow greater speed.

Speed work on court is perhaps the most effective means of developing speed for squash, as it demands the correct footwork, an essential skill for quick and efficient movement. However, court time is not always available and is usually best spent using a ball.

Drills to increase the speed of movement of your feet are also important, as they enhance your brain's ability to send signals to the correct musculature. Speed skipping is one such method, while an even more effective method involves running across a series of tyres, making sure to to put your feet in the holes of each tyre. You can then vary the holes in which you tread with successive runs, to practise reacting to different situations. Other drills of running on the spot (imagining yourself to be barefoot on hot cinders) will help increase the skill of fast movement. These should be blended into the programme in conjunction with the court drills, especially when moving towards the more important competitions in the season.

MOBILITY AND FLEXIBILITY

The range of exercises shown should be used for both warm-up and development of flexibility. Before and after playing or training, static stretching is best. Hold the stretch in the position shown, giving a mild sensation of discomfort. The stretch should be held for a minimum of 10 seconds, but more realistically for 20 to 30 seconds. Relax for a few seconds and then repeat.

To develop flexibility, stretching should be performed as a session in its own right, after some gentle pulse raising. Here the stretches should be held for a minimum of 30 seconds, up to 2 minutes if static stretching is the chosen mode. PNF stretching can also be used, which works on the stretch reflex of the muscle. There are a number of ways of using this type of technique, but all rely on muscle pairs, for example quadriceps and hamstrings. The ideal is to stretch the hamstring muscle first, then contract the quad muscles quite hard. This allows the hamstring muscles to relax more, whereupon a greater stretch is then allowed. Another method is to stretch a muscle, contract it in stretched position for at least 8 seconds, then stretch again, this time a little further. These methods are most useful in developing flexibility.

CORRECT EATING AND DRINKING

Nutrition can play a vital part in sports performance, the finer details of which could comprise a book in their own right. However, rather than look for an ergogenic effect from nutrition, the astute player will make sure that nutritional intake is sufficient to avoid problems in playing and training. In general a mixed diet is sufficient for the player, as long as you take in sufficient calories to match the demands of your activity. At least 60 per cent of your calories should come from carbohydrate, preferably in a complex form, such as bread, rice, pasta and potatoes. When you play and train, you utilize your body's limited stores of carbohydrate, which must be replaced, otherwise you will be running on an empty tank for your next bout of activity. The most effective time to replace this carbohydrate is within 30 to 60 minutes after you have finished the activity. This may mean you need to be organized if you do not live close enough to where you play and train. Try to get in the habit of it least having a carbohydrate snack, such as a banana or muesli bar, soon after your activity.

Another crucial aspect of nutrition is fluid. If you lose 2 per cent of your bodyweight in fluid, your performance will be impaired. Therefore it makes good sense to make sure that you are well hydrated before training and playing; as well as topping up at suitable opportunities, for example between games in a match. Sports drinks are ideal – do not experiment before or during a big match – otherwise water is quite acceptable. The best prepared players can often be seen with a bottle of drink near or with them at a tournament.

127

NO-RUSH CIRCUIT

For the no-rush circuit there is no time limit. Start with ten reps of each exercise to form a set. For progression add to the number of reps in each set over successive weeks until you can do twenty reps; then drop the number of reps down to ten and add to the number of sets and so on.

(The diagrams show the start position and the position you move to in the exercise.)

1 Short sit-up

Keeping your feet firmly on the floor, lift your shoulders up to a 30–40 degree angle and hold for one second before returning back down.

In this exercise and number 4, rest your hands lightly on the side of your head; if need be, put your thumbs in your ears! It is important that you do not pull your head up, as this can damage the knee and spine.

2 Back arches

Keep your legs crossed and feet firmly on the floor. Keep your head in a neutral position – that is, neck in line with your spine.

3 Back extension

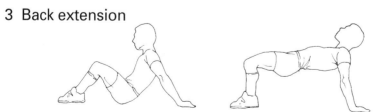

Aim to keep your head in a neutral position as you raise your backside. Keep your torso square with the floor.

4 Speed cramp

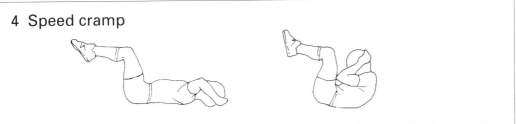

With your feet held up, raise your elbows touch your knees. This should be done in a fast, continuous motion.

5 Gluteal exercise

Your weight should be on your forearms and non-exercising knee. The exercising leg should kick forward and back continuously.

6 Sit-up

Simply slide the hands up the thighs to touch the knees and return in a controlled fashion.

ANAEROBIC CONDITIONING EXERCISES

Perform ten high speed reps of six of the following exercises in succession to form one circuit. Progressively add reps or sets. Vary the exercises used.

A Split jumps

While in the air swap the lead leg before landing.

B Squat jumps

Aim for maximum height in mid-air and change lead leg before landing.

C Jumping jacks

You should be able to clap your hands in the air before landing and jumping back to the start position.

D Calf raises

Keeping your balance, simply raise body by standing on toes and come down in a controlled fashion. Train calves both eccentrically and concentrically.

E Half squat

To strengthen quads. Raise heels slightly and keep back straight at all times. There should be a 90 degree angle at the knees.

F Squat thrust

A fast continuous movement which trains the legs to keep driving.

G Knee to toe

This exercise trains the quads with both eccentric and concentric muscular contractions. Alternate legs are bent, so that the knee sits next to the opposite foot.

H Press-ups

Keep the head, neck and spine in a straight line throughout.

To work triceps (back of upper arm) rest hands on step or bench as shown. Keeping legs straight, bend arms so that backside is lower, then push up back to start position.

I Push-ups

STRENGTH PROGRAMME

For pure strength perform two to four sets of just four or five reps, allowing a minimum of 2–3 minutes for recovery between sets, in a slow controlled manner with as much resistance as you can manage.

1 Power clean

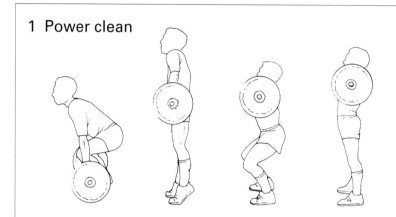

An excellent all-round body exercise that develops strength and power in legs, back, shoulders and arms. Perform in explosive fashion. Position 1: shoulders slightly over bar with feet on the ground, beneath bar, close to shins. Keep back straight and head up. Position 2: legs at full extension and arms still straight. Position 3: knees bent as the bar has been 'caught' resting on top of chest. Position 4: Breathe out as you finally straighten legs.

Remember: Keep your back straight when lowering bar.

2 Bench press

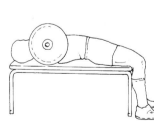
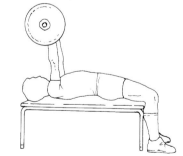

2. This is better done with free weights, although machines are safer if you're alone. Lower the bar slowly to the chest and breathe out as you push the bar up. This develops both arm and chest muscles.

3 Squat

An excellent exercise for quadriceps and hip flexors. Keep the feet apart, with the bar resting on your shoulders. Keep your back straight and head upright at all times. In lowest position, the thighs should be parallel to the floor.

4 Leg press

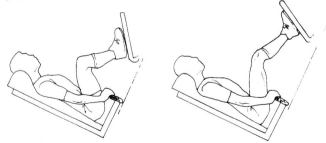

Machines can vary widely for leg press. You must have your back in a comfortable position and keep your neck relaxed. Push hard, but let the weight drop in a controlled fashion.

STRETCHING

For your warm-up hold static stretches for a minimum of 10 seconds in a position giving mild discomfort, relax, then repeat. To develop flexibility and warm-down hold stretches for between 30 seconds and 2 minutes.

1

This is a simple stretch for your triceps and the top of your shoulders. Put your arms overhead and then hold the elbow of one arm with the hand of the other arm and gently pull the elbow behind your head to create a stretch.

2

Stand with knees slightly bent and gently pull your elbow behind your head as you bend from your hips to the side.

3

Reach overhead and interlace your fingers with palms upward. Push your arms up and back slightly. Hold this stretch for 15 seconds but do not hold your breath.

4

Stretch your calves by leaning on a support with your forearms and resting your head on your hands. Bend one leg placing the foot on the ground in front of you with the other leg straight behind. Now slowly move your hips forward, keeping your lower back flat. Be sure to keep the heel of the straight leg on the ground, with toes pointed straight ahead or slightly turned in as you hold the stretch. Hold an easy stretch for 30 seconds.

Stretch the muscles in the front of the hip by moving one leg forward until the knee of the forward leg is directly over the ankle and the other knee rests on the floor. Without changing the position of the knee on the floor or the forward foot, lower the front of your hip downward to create an easy stretch. Hold for 30 seconds. You should feel this stretch in the front of the hip and possibly in the hamstrings and groin. This is excellent for lower back problems.

5

6

Lie on your back and relax with your knees bent and soles of your feet together. This comfortable exercise will stretch your groin. Hold it for 30 seconds letting gravity do the stretching. A variation is to gently rock your legs as one unit back and forth about ten to twelve times. These should be really easy movements of no more than 1inch (2.5cm) in either direction. Initiate the movements from the top of the hips.

7

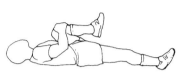

Lie on your back and pull your right leg towards your chest. For this stretch keep the back of your head on the floor or mat if possible, but don't strain. Hold an easy stretch for 30 seconds. Repeat, pulling your left leg toward your chest. Be sure to keep your lower back flat.

8

Start in a standing position with your feet about shoulder width apart and pointed straight ahead. Slowly bend forward from the hips, always keeping your knees slightly bent during the stretch so the lower back is not stressed. Let your neck and arms relax. Go to the point where you feel a slight stretch in the back of your legs. Stretch in this easy phase for 15 – 25 seconds, until you are relaxed. Do not stretch with knees locked or bounce when you stretch. Simply hold an easy stretch. Stretch by how you feel and not by how far you can go.

9

Place the back of your heel on a support about waist high. The leg on the ground should be slightly bent at the knee, with your foot pointed forwards as in a proper running or walking position. Now, while looking straight ahead, slowly bend forwards at the waist until you feel a good stretch in the back of the raised leg. Hold and relax. Find the easy stretch, relax, and then increase it. This is very good for running or walking.

10

Lie on your back with knees bent and feet flat on the floor. Roll your legs and hips over to one side and hold for 5 seconds then roll to the other side. Continue for 30 seconds.

11

Lie flat on your back, and bend the right knee over your left leg and down towards the floor. Press the right knee to the floor with your left hand while keeping the shoulder and left arm on the floor. Repeat on the other side.

11
Your Programme

To get better at squash it is important to think ahead and plan ahead. This book has concentrated on your squash skills (your technique, shots and skills). You get better at squash by having better skills.

We have also looked at all the factors that affect your performance (technical or skill, tactical, mental and physical). Your total performance is the sum of the performances in these areas. Imagine performing up to your best in each area and experiencing a peak performance.

The approach in this book has been developmental. We have emphasized developing your abilities in all areas. Development is a process that will happen over time. It may go in fits and starts or spurts and plateaus. You may hit limitations but these barriers can be pushed out with practice and training.

Squash players tend to have short-term objectives. They want to play well tomorrow or next week and find it hard to look ahead three months or a season. For this reason they tend to do the same thing each time they play rather than trying to work different things into their game. Practise something once or twice and it may not make an impact on your skills or game. You may even get worse. Practise it twenty times (for example the technique practice sequence) and you could well have considerable or dramatic improvement. Twenty times would be twice a week for ten weeks. If you lack stamina, start running daily: in one week you will be tired, in six weeks you will be fitter.

YOUR TRAINING SESSION

Squash is a brilliant game in which we compete with skills, tactical and mental abilities, and our fitness. Training to improve at the sport can involve several different activities in one session. Always start a session by warming up and stretching for 10 minutes at the beginning and warming down and stretching for at least 10 minutes at the end. The stretching at the beginning of the session should use 10-second stretches and at the end 30-second stretches, which will help develop flexibility and mobility.

Work on skills at the beginning of a session and at fitness training afterwards. You need to be fresh to get the benefit of skill training. If you are a bit fatigued from the skill training you can still get the benefit of fitness training. If you are working on speed in a composite session this must be done when you are fresh and before any endurance work.

PLANNING A PROGRAMME

Your overall programme is a combination of your squash and fitness training and competitions

Work out what your goals are. Your programme must provide realistic steps towards these. Write your programme down. Record your results so that you can see exactly what you are doing. Evaluate and revise as necessary.

Sit down with your coach and decide what skills you need. What are you going to do and when? Firstly look at your competitive goals and obligations. When do you have tournaments and team or club matches? Secondly fit your practices and practice matches around these. Thirdly fit in your fitness activities.

A Balanced Programme

A balance programme will cover each area and try to provide the correct balance between practice and play, between squash and fitness training and between work and rest.

Vary your fitness activities between strength, speed, aerobic and anaerobic activities so that, for example, you are not working on strength on consecutive days. Flexibility must be a daily routine before and after each session or match.

A Progressive Programme

The practice progression moves from solo to pairs practice, to condition games, to practice games, to matches.

Slowly build up your fitness in the same way. Traditional theory emphasizes working progressively from strength through to aerobic endurance to anaerobic endurance and then to speed. In squash don't think of these as absolute bands but as changes of emphasis. For example, a little bit of speed could be combined in a conditioning session, which would keep you in touch with

speed and include anaerobic endurance and then some anaerobic endurance. As you move to the competitive stage the emphasis of the sessions can change.

A Long-term Programme

The long-term programme allows you to build up to playing competitively. You can work on parts of your game without immediately having to put them into effect in matches. A long-term programme allows you to build up your strength and stamina, which may slow you down slightly in the short term. Speed and agility can be added before competition. Your match and 'maintenance' programme will then maintain fitness throughout the competitive stage.

Phases

1. *Regeneration* At the end of the season take a break from squash so that you can enter training mentally fresh. Make this an active recovery, partaking in activities that you enjoy and that will help build fitness. Perhaps they will be swimming, cycling or mountain biking. This is something you could do for several weeks.

2. *Foundation (six to eight weeks)* Squash training here may concentrate on basic technique, on improving skills and developing new skills. This is not always easy to do during competition and this is your chance to work at it. Fitness training will concentrate on building cardio-vascular fitness and strength.

3. *Preparation* Squash training moves to pairs and condition games and then into practice games and matches just before competition.

137

4. *Competition* Squash training concentrates on matches. Practise skills and movement so they are at a peak for competition. Fitness training is on a maintenance programme but emphasizes speed, agility and movement. Make sure you are fresh for competition. Rest is important.

Levels

Beginner It is hard to improve at squash playing once a week. A club player should be on court a minimum of three times a week and this is what a beginner should build up to. Initially try to practise at least once a week. Try to obtain coaching and use it in conjunction with the practices in this book.

Club Player You must play at least three times a week. Put some time aside for solo practice and if possible get a regular practice partner or do a squad practice session.

A good rule is to do some fitness activity on the days you are not playing. If lack of fitness is a factor in your game, building up basic stamina in the summer will be very useful. Regular and hard games will also help raise your fitness level.

Competitive Player You need to set out your goals, organization and programme. Plan your season, foundation, preparation and competition.

Five sessions a week is about the right level. Play three times a week, which leaves two fitness sessions a week. Off season you will be able to play less and train more. As an alternative to three matches you could, for example, play two matches and make up a session with one half-hour practice and then a gym session or a circuit.

Professional With your coach work out the areas in your game that you need to develop. Work out a long-term programme for them. Fit this in with your medium-term competitive targets.

SAMPLE PROGRAMMES

Example schedule for a club player

Days

1 Club night + aerobic endurance.

2 Solo practice + anaerobic endurance or combination session.

3 Club match.

4 Rest.

5 League match.

6 Rest.

7 Pairs practice + strength and power.

Example schedule for a professional

Day	a.m	p.m	Evening
1	Pairs	Aerobic	
2	Solo		Hard play
3	Aerobic	Pairs	
4	Pairs	Solo/ easy play	Gym. Strength
5	Solo	Med/ Hard play	Aerobic
6	Free Day		
7	Solo	Easy play	Circuits gym

A Sample Twenty-week Programme

This number of activities would be the maximum recommended and would need to be scaled down for club and competitive players. However, many of the ingredients could be combined into a session or a day.

Sample 20 Week Training Programme

Week	Aerobic Endurance	Strength & Power	Condition Circuit	Anaerobic Endurance	Speed	Matches	Solo Practice	Pairs Practice
1	3	2	2			1	2+	
2	3	2	2			1	2+	
3	3+	2	2			1	3+	
4	4+	2	2			1	3+	
5	4	1	1			1	2	
6	4	1	1			1	2	
7	3	1	1	1		1	1	1
8	3	1	1	1		1	1	1
9	2	1	1	2		1	1	2
10	2	1	1	2		1	1	2
11	2	1	1	3		1	1	3
12	2	1	1	3		1	1	3
13	1+	1	1	2	2	2	2	2
14	1+	1	1	2	2	2	1	2
15	1+	1	1	2	2	2	1	2
16	1+	1	1	2	2	2	1	2
17	1			1	1	3	1	1
18	1			1	1	3	1	1
19	1			1	1	3	1	1
20	1			1	1	3	1	1

Useful Addresses

World Squash Federation (WSF)
6 Havelock Road
Hastings
East Sussex
TN34 1BP
Tel: 01424 429245
Fax: 01424 429250

The Squash Player Magazine
Longhouse
460 Bath Road
Longford
Middlesex
UB7 0EB
Tel: 01753 775511
Fax: 01753 775512

Squash Rackets Association (SRA)
Westpoint
33/34 Warple Way
Acton
London
W3 0RQ
Tel: 0181 746 1616
Fax: 0181 746 0580

Index

Advanced pressure exercises, 101–2
Aiming, 29–30
Analysing matches, 103
Anxiety, 115–16
Arousal curve, 115
Attacking game, 108–9

Back corners, 63–6
Balance, 14–16
Ball control, 10–12
Boast, 60–2, 64–6

Clinger, 44
Coaching, 9, 95–101
    the coach, 95–6
    coaching progression, 98–9
    course structure, 96–7
    lesson structure, 96
Combinations, 107–13
Concentration, 116–17
Court, 8
    coverage, 102
    movement, 30–1
Cut, 67–8

Deception, 69–70
Defensive game, 105
Disguise, 68
Distance from the ball, 14
Drop, 58–60
Dying, 44
Dying length, 43

Extra width, 72

Fault finding, 32–3
Faults, 30
Fitness, 118–35
    aerobic endurance, 118–19
    anaerobic endurance, 119–20
    eating and drinking, 127
Flexibility, 120
Footwork, 14
Freeze check, 16

Game plan, 112–13
Grip
    grip check, 18
    V grip, 17
    wobble check, 17
Group coaching, 101

Height, 44

Length, 43
Levels, 138
Lob, 51–2, 71–2
Loose, 44

Match preparation, 113, 117
Methods of coaching, 99–100
Mistakes, 103–5
Movement, 36–8
    changing direction, 36–7
    turning, 36
Movement control, 12–13

Nick, 44

Opponent, 112

Paths, 35–6
Percentage squash, 110–11
Placement, 42–4
  length, 43
  width, 44
Positional game, 106–8
Positioning, 13
Practices
  back corners, 65
  boast, 62
  condition game, 91–2
  court movement, 37–8
  crosscourt, 51
  drive, 83–5
  drop, 60
  front court practices, 80–2
  kill, 63
  lob, 52
  pairs, 86–9, 94
  practice games, 93–4
  practice session, 79
  return of serve, 56–7
  scoring, 91
  sequences, 83–5
  service, 55
  shadow practice, 37
  solo, 79–85
  squash movement, 38
  straight drive, 48
  technique, 38–40
  threes and fours, 89–90
  two pairs, 90–1
  volley, 82–3
Preparation, 28–9
Pressure game, 105–6

Racket, 8
  control, 17–20
  edge, 21
  face, 20–1
Ready position, 34
Recovery, 35

Service
  return of serve, 55–7, 107
  rules, 52–3
  types of service, 54–5
Short, 44
Shots
  backcorner boast, 64
  backcorner straight drive, 64–5
  back wall boast or lob, 71–2
  boast, 60–2
  cling or narrow lob, 72
  corkscrew lob, 75
  crosscourt drive, 48–51
  crosscourt volley nick, 75
  drop, 58–60
  flick lob, 71
  floating boast, 73
  kill, 62–3
  lob, 51–2
  return of serve, 55–6
  reverse angle, 62
  service, 52–5
  skid boast, 72
  straight drive, 44–8
  straight volley drop, 74
  volley, 57–8
  volley kill, 75
Skills tests, 76–8
Speed, 120
Spin
  cut, 67–8
  topspin, 68
Squash action, 22
Stance
  back corner, 16
  basic, 15–16
  open, 16
Strength and power, 120, 125
Surprise, 68–9
Swing, 21–2
  compact, 22–5
  developing your swing, 28–9

full, 25–8
  racket paths, 25
  racket speed, 28
  short, 25
  swing size, 25

Tactical balance, 109–10
Tactics, 102–13
Technique, 10–41
  ball control, 10–12
  court movement, 30–1
  movement control, 12–13
  racket control, 17
Temperament, 114–17
Tight, 44
Timing, 28–9
Touch, 68
Training
  aerobic, 123
  anaerobic, 123, 124–5
  circuit, 124–6
  conditioning exercises, 130–1

ghosting, 37–8, 122
  movement, 127
  no-rush circuit, 128–9
  non-specific training, 123–4
  shadow, 37
  specific training, 121–3
  speed, 126–7
  strength, 132–3
  stretching, 134–5

Variations, 70–1
Volley, 57–8

Watching, 29
Weak shots, 102
Width, 44
Wrist
  cocked wrist, 19–20
  wrist action, 22

Your programme, 136–9